It's All About Me!

Stories & Insights from the *Geese*

GREG **"Geese"** GIESEN

Award-winning author of
Mondays At 3

A Greg Giesen Publication

© 2019 by Greg Giesen. All rights reserved.
First edition.

Printed and bound in the USA by
Greg Giesen
Denver, Colorado 80209
720-323-1551
www.LeadingFromWithin.net

ISBN: 978-1-7923-1240-3

Cataloging in Publication Data is on file with
the Library of Congress

Book Cover Design by Creative Visions

To My Family and Friends

Thanks for being a significant part of my life . . .
and my stories.

Table of Contents

Introduction

*Maybe the journey isn't so much about becoming
anything. Maybe it's about unbecoming
everything that isn't really you so you can be
who you were meant to be in the first place.*

— Paulo Coelho

I have been both a student and teacher in the
professional development and self-help industry
my whole career. My transition from student to teacher surfaced
the moment I began writing about my experiences and sharing
the insights I gained from them. It was then that I realized I had
something to say that could benefit others.

This book is a collection of my most memorable stories and
insights from the past 40 years. The stories are all true and the
insights are as meaningful to me today as they were when I first
had them. Because I use many of these stories and teachings in my
talks and presentations around the country, I decided it was time
to put them all together into one place.

I must admit, I've really enjoyed reflecting, writing, and re-
experiencing the moments in this book. It gave me a new appreciation for the journey I'm on, and a renewed desire to keep this
process going. Expect to read more from me in the future.

It is my hope that these stories and insights will speak to each of you and provide a thought or two to ponder. More importantly, I hope my work will encourage you to consider writing your own story. The power of a story is eternal, and can be passed on from generation to generation, whether through writing, video, audio, or any other forms of creative expression. This book is now part of my legacy, just as your story is a part of yours.

I included a bonus chapter at the end of the book featuring my Eight Simple Rules to Managing Conflict. The stories and insights within those eight simple rules have been very meaningful to me and I wanted to share them with you as well.

As part of my writing style, I've added dialogue to many of the stories. I used this technique to personalize the stories and create greater flow across the storyline. I took the liberty to ad-lib some comments, in cases where I couldn't recall exactly what was said or by whom. Let's call it creative freedom. I also changed the names in most of the stories for privacy purposes.

The stories can be read in any order you desire. Feel free to pick and choose.

I'd love to hear your thoughts. Perhaps you'd like to share one of your stories. My email is greg.giesen@me.com and my website is www.leadingfromwithin.net. Drop a line when you get a chance.

Authentically,
Geese

1
Conflict on the Mountain

The two most important days in your life are the day
you are born ... and the day you find out why.
— Mark Twain

It was about 4:30 a.m. when Christian, our instructor, rousted us from our tents. It was the eighth day of a grueling 10-day Outward Bound program and we faced the ultimate challenge: we were to summit Mount Massive by noon and return to camp before dusk. At 14,421 feet high, Mount Massive is the second-highest peak in Colorado and the third-highest peak in the United States. It was a 14-mile round-trip hike, so we had our work cut out for us.

After a quick breakfast and pep talk by Christian, we were off on our journey, backpacks strapped on, and flashlights guiding our every step.

The first half of the climb went flawlessly. It was especially exhilarating to experience the sunrise, and the resulting warmth on our faces as we slowly weaved through a field of aspen trees. Everything was just so beautiful.

But then, without warning, a loud cry echoed through the trees. I followed the sound and saw Valerie rolling on the ground, clutching her ankle.

"Are you okay?" screamed David, as he rushed toward her.

"I'm fine; don't worry about me," Valerie called, loud enough so others wouldn't keep repeating the same question. Valerie was a trooper, and she wanted to reach the top of Mount Massive as much as anyone. In fact, aside from me, the other nine participants were from outside of Colorado and had never climbed a *fourteener*. For them, succeeding was not just a physical challenge; it gave them major bragging rights when they returned home. So, reaching the summit was not an option—it was a mandate.

For the next hour or so, Valerie downplayed her injury, although her slight hobble had become a very noticeable limp. The group's pace had slowed significantly and sometimes we had to stop as Valerie tried to regain her composure. "I'll get through this," she kept saying to anyone who would listen.

Before long, the rest of the group was exchanging glances and expressing concern and frustration. It was becoming apparent that our goal of reaching the summit was in jeopardy; yet no one wanted to admit or entertain that possibility. Finally, Jonathan broke the silence. "This is not working!" he said. The group gathered around.

"Then go without me," Valerie said. Tears welled up in her eyes.

"Hold on a second," said Kelly, Valerie's closest friend. "This is a group decision."

Within seconds we were arguing over our options, and what was the "right" thing to do. Voices were raised, people were talking over each other, and no one was listening. We were fighting on the mountain. Half the group was pushing to abort the hike and take Valerie back to camp; while the other half, including Valerie, wanted to press on, albeit at a much slower pace.

All the while, Christian watched from afar, curious to see how the group dynamics would play out. Finally, after no progress, he approached us. "I can see this is an important discussion to have right now," he said. "But I'd like to suggest that you move this conversation to a new location," as he pointed to a different spot on the mountain.

Our group was so engrossed in our dilemma that we acquiesced. We got up, and kept arguing as we moved to the spot Christian had chosen. Even our semicircle seemed to stay intact. Interestingly, no one, including myself, questioned his request for us to move. Clearly, we were completely oblivious to our surroundings and his guidance.

Christian, on the other hand, was very aware. He knew the mountain very well and noticed that in our initial attempt to problem solve, we had all positioned ourselves in a semicircle that faced *down* the mountain. We were primarily looking at where we had been, not where we were headed. Even our conversation had a downward, negative energy—as we assigned blame, took sides, and felt divided.

But now, instead of facing down toward the base of Mount Massive, Christian had moved us to a spot that faced uphill, with the sun radiating off the summit. It was the most spectacular sight I'd ever seen. It also was the first time any of us had seen the top of the mountain that day. From our new angle, we could see the trail all the way to the top, making the remaining distance seem much more doable than we imagined. I could not only see the summit, I could smell it, taste it, and almost touch it. I could visualize being at the top.

Without any acknowledgment of what had changed, the group dynamics shifted instantaneously. All of our blaming, arguing, and negativity were replaced with excitement, amazement, and optimism. Our conversation moved from debating two options to a synergistic conversation on how to summit with Valerie setting the pace.

It's amazing that Christian never explained his actions on the mountain that day. And yet, his subtle gesture of changing the backdrop of our discussion, provided the most profound insight and lesson around the importance of vision that I've ever experienced.

I am also happy to report that the whole group successfully summited Mount Massive, just minutes before an afternoon storm engulfed us. We accomplished this by carrying all of Valerie's gear for her and having her lead the group all the way up to the top.

In the end, reaching the summit wasn't nearly as significant for me as the transformation that we, as a group, went through in order to get there. We couldn't have made it without Christian's gentle guidance, and without the powerful vision of Mount Massive appearing as we bickered on the mountain.

On that day, I learned many lessons about leadership that I will never forget. Specifically:

1. I learned the importance of having a vision; a vision that is so alive that it penetrates every pore.
2. I learned that groups handle adversity better when there is an overriding vision and purpose that unites them.
3. I learned the significance of focusing on *where we're headed* (as an individual, group, or organization) versus *where we've been.*

And most importantly,

4. I learned that leadership through action can be more powerful than leadership through words.

Sometimes it may take 14,421 feet in order to learn an important lesson, but trust me, it's worth every step.

2
Bless Me Father . . .

*I am convinced that life is 10% what happens
to me and 90% how I react to it.*

— Charles Swindoll

In 2014, I went to a Halloween party dressed as a priest. Actually, I went to the wrong Halloween party in 2014 dressed as a priest. It turns out, there were two houses right next door to each other having parties and I, having never been to my friend's house before, walked into the wrong one.

And then things got interesting.

Since I was so sure I was at the right house, I decided to simply let myself in, bypassing proper protocols like knocking on the door or ringing the doorbell. After all, these were my friends.

Upon entering, I was greeted by a little eight-year-old girl who happily took my coat. *That's odd,* I thought to myself, *I didn't know there would be kids at this party.*

Then I surveyed the room, searching for a familiar face. There were none. Actually, I thought I recognized the people dressed as Count Dracula and Catwoman, but neither seemed to recognize me. There was also a group gathered in the kitchen, but aside from a couple of bad imitations of Johnny Depp's pirate character, I recognized no one.

Usually in these awkward moments, the party host or hostess will surface and welcome their guest (in this case, me) into the party, but no such luck. No one emerged. It also occurred to me that I had never met my friend's friends before.

I suddenly was a little self-conscious. There I was, dressed in a priest's outfit, standing aimlessly in the hallway, surrounded by goblins, ghosts, and shady characters. I felt like an extra in a horror movie, called in to perform some kind of exorcism. Oh yeah, and apparently, I also was invisible. No one spoke to me.

I needed to do something, I reasoned, so I did what anyone would do in this situation. I headed for my safe haven—better known as the bar.

I don't know if you've ever worn a priest outfit to a party before, but it can be an interesting experience to say the least. As I walked over to the bar area of the (wrong) house, I noticed people (who I didn't know) respectfully moved out of my way as I passed. You know, kind of like the parting of the Red Sea. What's more, many nodded and said, "Father" as I went by. And I nodded back, like I was blessing them or something. Weird.

I grabbed a beer (I know, it should have been wine) and chatted with the Shakespeare character standing next to me. Within seconds, he asked for some advice on a personal situation, like we've known each other for years—or like I'm a real priest! I gladly gave my two cents, just happy to have someone to talk with.

Moments later another guy in a robe comes in from having had a cigarette on the back porch and says to me, "It was so strange out there. I was hearing voices."

Are you telling me this because I look like a priest, I thought. I laughed awkwardly, hoping he'd go away. He did.

Eventually a cavewoman found her way to me. "So how do you know Paul?" she asked.

I said, "I know Karen."

"Who's Karen?" she replied.

"Karen, the host of the party."

"This party?" she asked with a confused look on her face.

"Isn't this Karen's house?" I asked, as if the floor was about to give way beneath my feet.

"No, this is Paul's house. I think you might be at the wrong party!"

In that moment I could see heads turn toward me as the room became uncomfortably silent.

"This isn't 3757 Briarwood?" I joked, already knowing the answer.

"No, this is 3755."

"But we'd love to have you stay, Father!" yelled one of the Johnny Depps.

"Why not, you're already here," added Catwoman.

If there ever was a time for an exorcist, this was probably it. I smiled as my face turned bright red. Even the guy in the devil's outfit looked pale in comparison.

"I should probably make an appearance next door," I mused, as I backed out of the kitchen. "But I'm sure I'll be back."

My walk to the coat room and out the front door couldn't have happened fast enough as I humbly hightailed it to the party next door.

This time, I rang the doorbell. Karen welcomed me in.

"You look like you've seen a ghost," she said, leading the way.

"You have no idea," I said and headed for the bar (again).

3
A Defining Moment

My high school counselor looked concerned. "You're a follower, Greg. You do just enough to get by with little to no ambition. I'd be lying if I didn't say that I'm worried about you. Tell me again where you're going to school?"

"Western State," I said.

"And what was it about Western that attracted you?" He seemed to anticipate what I would say next.

"I don't know," I sheepishly responded. "A bunch of guys from the soccer team are going."

"You see Greg, that's what I mean. You need to think about what *you* want to get out of the college experience. Do it for you, not for your friends."

I knew where he was going with the pep talk, but I just didn't care. In my family, going to college was not just an option, it was required. And as fortunate as I was to be in that position, I had absolutely no idea what I wanted from a college education, let alone a career. At that point in my life, all I seemed to care about was having fun, meeting women, and playing soccer. Nothing else really mattered.

My Freshman and Sophomore Years

My high school counselor was right: I was a follower. I did whatever my buddies wanted to do and went wherever they wanted to go. It wasn't long before a group of us on the soccer team bonded and formed a little social clique. We went everywhere together and most evenings we wound up in one of our dorm rooms watching Johnny Carson, eating Ritz crackers, and drinking beer. Although we weren't *nerds,* per se, you could hardly say we fit in. Outside of soccer, hanging out, and going to parties, my first two years came and went as fast as it gets cold in Gunnison. And to nobody's surprise, my GPA at the end of my sophomore year was a very unstable 2.0. And that was after taking all the easy classes.

And then the oddest thing happened. Toward the end of sophomore year, the three captains of the women's soccer team paid me a visit.

"We've got a favor to ask you," said one of them.

"The answer is no," I replied jokingly, still trying to figure out what they could possibly want with me.

"We want you to be our head soccer coach next year," said another.

All I could do is laugh. "Now that's funny. Who put you up to this? Was it Jon? Alan? You ladies are such a hoot."

"We're serious," said the third captain. "We thought you'd be a good coach."

"Me? Why me?" I assumed their initial choices must have turned them down. "What about Dave or Alan? They are much better players than I am."

The women refused to back down. They cited my organizational and leadership abilities, and how easy I was to work with. Their case was actually impressive—to anyone but me. They painted a picture of someone I didn't recognize. Someone I didn't think I could be. I was torn on so many levels.

"Can I think about it?" I said. I hoped that maybe they'd come to their senses and ask someone else.

They reluctantly agreed and went on their way, leaving me in a state of quandary. *Why me? Why now?* was all I could think. That night in the shower I recall looking up into the heavens and thinking, *What do they see in me that I don't?*

It was at that moment, that *defining moment*, that my life took a drastic turn.

I was ready to go into my third year of college—just as I had entered my first two—with little focus and hoping things would eventually figure themselves out. But that was before the coaching request. Suddenly I had another path to consider. *Could I step up and be someone who belongs at the front, leading, rather than hiding toward the back? Do I have what it takes to be a head coach? Do I even know what to do?*

The defining moment for me wasn't so much the request to coach as it was the intense self-evaluation that followed. I had to be willing to see the world, and my existence in it, from a new perspective. I had to see in myself what the three captains already had seen.

Over that summer I began to embrace my role as the head coach. I was in uncharted waters, but I started planning the season, organizing the practices, and, when the season began, leading the team. It was exhilarating to step out of the shadows and become the confident, supportive, and effective leader I was meant to be.

My Junior and Senior Years

To my initial surprise, I liked being in a leadership role and I thoroughly enjoyed being a coach. In fact, I liked it so much, that I also took on the additional role of co-coaching the men's team. And that was just the beginning. During the next two years, I became a writer for the college newspaper, started a psychology club on campus, and worked as a peer advisor assisting and mentoring freshman students.

I discovered a side of me that had been dormant all my life. I was motivated to get involved, lead, and make a difference in the lives of others. What's more, instead of selecting the easiest classes, as I did my first two years, I sought out the challenging professors so I could learn more. I also ran for student body president my senior year and won! By the time I graduated, I had raised my GPA from 2.0 to 2.95, getting all As and one B in four semesters.

Talk about a turnaround! I was transformed during my four years at Western. And those extracurricular experiences helped me land a full-ride graduate assistantship at Miami University.

Afterthoughts

Reflecting back on my college years, I am so grateful that the three captains of the women's soccer team saw my potential and put their faith in me. It sparked a much needed defining moment that changed my life forever.

It's amazing how a simple nudge can make such a difference.

4

Introducing President Carter

If it scares you, it is probably worth giving it a try.

— Seth Godin

When I think back on my time as director of student activities at the University of Redlands, there is one memory that always will rise above the rest. It's a memory that still brings chills up and down my spine. Perhaps because it involved a number of *firsts*.

It was the first time I spoke at the historic Memorial Chapel on the University of Redlands campus.

It was the first time I spoke in front of more than 200 people.

It was the first time I spoke to the University community, alumni, and dignitaries all together in one place.

It was the first time I wrote and presented an introduction for a famous person.

It was the first time I met a president of the United States.

It was the first time I had an intimate one-on-one dinner with a president of the United States.

It was the first time I rode in the president's limo.

But it wasn't the first time that I got so nervous that I thought I was going to pass out.

The Request

I thought it was pretty cool that President Carter accepted our request to speak at the University. I've booked a lot of famous speakers, artist, musicians, and authors, but never a president of the United States. This was the cherry on top of the cake, as far as I was concerned. But little did I know what was coming next:

John (Student Body President): "Hey, do you have a minute?"

Me: "Of course. What's up?"

John: "I wanted to ask you something. Actually, it's not just me, the executive team wanted me to ask you on behalf of the whole group."

Me: "Okay, shoot," I said, wondering what could be so important.

John: "We thought it would be appropriate for you to introduce President Carter at the convocation next month."

Me: "What? Who? Me? Why me?"

John: "Now that's the confidence I like to see," he said jokingly. "Yes you. You did all the work to bring him here and you deserve the credit."

Me: "But it's a student event. Don't you think it should be a student who introduces him?"

John: "I've already talked to President Appleton, and he thought it was a good idea too. So, it's decided. You'll be introducing President Carter!" John smiled and gave me the thumbs up gesture as he walked out of my office.

I could only shake my head and wonder: *What just happened here?*

The Good . . . the Bad . . . and the Ugly

You know when someone says to you, "Don't think about pink elephants," and you can only think about pink elephants? You're thinking about pink elephants now, aren't you? See, it works. Well, that's what happened to me once I agreed to introduce President Carter, only the pink elephants were replaced by stage fright, anxiety, and pure fear. I mean, it is one thing to stand up in front of my Toastmasters group of 13 to give a speech. It's an entirely different challenge to introduce a president of the United States in front a packed Memorial Chapel of more than 1,200 people.

I began obsessing about it. I'd frequently wake up it in the middle of the night in a cold sweat after dreaming about it. And, of course, everywhere I went people asked me about it. "Aren't you nervous?" they'd say, or, "Do you realize how many people are going to be there?"

On top of all the comments, my mind was going crazy as I prepared. *Should I use humor or just tell the facts? Do I talk about his presidency, or all the things he's done afterward? Can I read my introduction? And who's going to be in the audience? Does it matter? What do 1,200 people look like from the podium up on the stage? And what if I mess up?*

As the event got closer, my anxiety compounded. I was having a difficult time pretending that I was ready, when I knew deep down inside that I wasn't even close. Fortunately, I was scheduled as one of the speakers for my Toastmaster club a couple of days before the convocation. This would be my opportunity to practice my introduction for the president and get some last-minute feedback from people I really trusted.

The Practice Speech

Bob Graham, the Toastmaster of the meeting, cleared his throat. "And now I'd like to introduce to you, Greg Giesen. Greg will be presenting his introduction for President Carter. He welcomes your feedback at the end of his speech. Please help me welcome, Greg Giesen!"

The eight members who decided to show up that day applauded.

Despite the small audience, I was trembling uncontrollably. *What's going on! Why am I so freaking nervous?*

Sweat began dripping down my face. My voice shook more than the "L" in Chicago going around a curve.

The crowd of eight looked startled, wondering what they could do to help.

Finally, after a couple of minutes of pure agony on everyone's part, Randy, one of the members stood up and shouted, "Time out!"

I was relieved.

"Greg, what's going on?" he asked.

"What do you mean?" I replied. "I'm just a little nervous," still gasping for air.

"A little?" yelled Mary Ann, the club vice president. "Greg, you are dying up there. That's not like you."

The speech that I was trying to give had now worked its way to my stomach, and I was in agony. "Okay, I'm really nervous," I said. "I've never spoken in front of so many people, and I'm really uptight about it."

Seeing how important this moment was, Bob suggested we all sit in a circle and forego the rest of the structured meeting. He then softly looked at me and asked, "Greg, when you got up to the podium, were you seeing in your mind's eye this group of eight or were you seeing a crowd of people inside Memorial Chapel?"

Initially I thought that was a very odd question, but then I closed my eyes to see what I was seeing. My body tensed up as the image became more and more clear.

The room I saw wasn't a chapel at all. It was some kind of arena with rows and rows of people going as far back as I could

Photo by McCormick Company courtesy Amarillo Public Library

see; maybe one or two football fields long. It was massive! I saw myself as this little dot up on stage looking out into an infinite sea of people. I felt so alone up there, so intimidated, so disconnected.

I shook my head, trying to push the image out of my mind. "Oh my God, I wasn't even in this room! I wasn't even in the chapel. I was in some packed arena."

Bob nodded. "You weren't present with us in this room. That's where that *alone* and *disconnected* feeling comes from. You weren't here!"

Now I was nodding.

Ron jumped in. "You are one of the best speakers in this club. What makes you so good is your ability to connect with us during your speeches. Whether it's your humor or your stories or your eye contact, you have that ability to hook us in immediately." He paused. "And that didn't happen this time."

Mary Ann interrupted. "Greg, you always start your speeches with something funny. How come you didn't do that for this speech?"

I leaned in. "Mary Ann, actually I do have a couple of funny lines that I plan on using. I just don't like testing out my jokes ahead of time for some reason."

"Because they may not be funny?" joked John, another member. Everyone laughed.

"Timing," I said. "My jokes have to be fairly unrehearsed in order for them to have that impromptu aspect to them. If I think too much, or get feedback on a particular joke, it can lose its spontaneity and come off as too contrived."

"The jokes should help you get into the groove, but how else could you calm your nerves beforehand?" asked new member Dawn.

"I have a suggestion that should help," offered Bob. "Go into Memorial Chapel—today—and stand behind the podium and look out. Look up into the balcony and imagine people sitting there. Look to the two sides and see every seat filled. Look to the farthest seat in the back of the room and put a person there. Fill the whole chapel. Then breathe. Feel the floor, the crowd, and see President Carter on the side, waiting to come up. Breathe. Then break down the audience a little more. See the faces, both familiar and unfamiliar, the smiles, and feel the energy. Breathe in the energy and see it as your energy."

I was one big smile at this point. "I got it. This isn't about my speech and it isn't about my skills to deliver my speech. It's all about the image that I conjured up about the audience that's the problem. I simply don't know what 1,200 people in the chapel will look like, so my mind added a couple of zeros to the equation."

The group nodded and smiled.

"Bob," I asked, "Do you mind if I skip practicing again so I can head out to the chapel right now?"

Cheers and high fives broke out as I headed out the door. Nothing else needed to be said. Everyone there knew that I didn't need more practice. I needed to visualize.

The Chapel

I will always be grateful to Bob for the chapel suggestion. After standing on stage and looking out at all the empty seats, I saw how much my imagination had exaggerated things. When you divide a 1,200-seat facility into a left side, a right side, a middle section, and a balcony, the room gets very small and intimate. In fact, I was amazed at how close every seat was to the stage. Eye contact, even with the farthest person in the room, would be no problem.

Now this is very doable, I thought, as my confidence reemerged. *I'm going to knock the ball out of the park!*

And I did.

5
My Day at the Funeral Home . . . And How It Changed My Life Forever

> On the day of judgment, we shall not be asked
> what we have done but how much did we love.
>
> — Thomas à Kempis

Second Thoughts

It was 7:55 a.m. and I recall sitting in my car, which was parked out in front of the funeral home. My stomach felt a little queasy and I wondered if this was such a great idea after all. You see, I like to know firsthand what my clients do, and some of my clients happen to be in the funeral industry.

But wait, there's more to this rationale. I was curious. I was curious to know what kind of person would choose the funeral profession and why. I was curious to know what a typical day would look like at a funeral home, or if there ever was such a thing. And truthfully, I was curious to know what it would be like to be around dead bodies all day.

That sounded morbid, didn't it?

Actually, let me be more specific. I was curious to know if my views on life itself would change after spending a day helping out at a funeral home: a day which included working with both the living and the dead.

So that's why I was granted permission to be there. In fact, the owner was so appreciative that he promised to expose me to as much as he could during my day at his funeral home. And that's also why I didn't want to get out of the car. I was getting cold feet.

Just then a car pulled into the spot next to me. It was Harold Banes, the operations manager. My first meeting was to be with him.

He pointed toward the front door. "Come on in, Greg," he said smiling. "We've got a full day planned for you."

I greeted him nervously.

"Hey Harold. I'm looking forward to today," I mumbled. "But go easy on me. I'm a rookie."

"This is your first time?" he asked, looking surprised.

"Afraid so," I replied.

"Not to worry," he said. "I think you're going to get a real good sense of what goes on here on a typical day."

He led me through the lobby and down a set of stairs, to what's called the preparation room: a place equipped for preparing the deceased for final disposition. We headed over to one side and sat down at a desk with chairs. The room was very cold with bright lights shining down on us from above. I took in the details of the room. Along the walls were specially designed shelves reserved for the four bodies that were scheduled for viewings and needed some final touch up. I'll spare you the details, but let's just say it was going to be a very busy morning for the make-up artist.

"Are you okay?" asked Harold, seeing the shock on my face.

"I'm fine," I replied, knowing that I wasn't. "I just didn't expect to see all of this quite so soon."

"It is hard to get used to," he said. "But these aren't just corpses to us. Each body represents a life. A life with incredible stories and experiences. It's our job in this room to prepare these bodies for viewing, so that their loved ones see them looking at their best and in a state of peace. If we can do that, we've done our job."

Goosebumps tickled my arms. "Harold, I felt that," referring to what he just said. "You really are passionate about this."

"This isn't just a job to me," he said. "This is a calling. I'm here because I want to help people at one of the most difficult times in their lives. Ask around," he said, "you won't find anyone who's here because of the paycheck."

"But doesn't it get depressing being around so much death?" I asked.

He shook his head. "We serve the families, Greg, and they are very much alive."

As Harold continued to talk, my attention drifted over to the other side of the room where four bodies, covered with sheets from the neck down, lay peacefully. I remember feeling an overwhelming sadness as I tried to imagine their lives. Yet, at the same time, I felt grateful to be with them during this final phase of preparation. I wanted to reassure them that they were each being treated with the utmost respect and dignity at the end of their lives, and that they didn't need to worry. They were in good hands. They were in Harold's hands.

"Greg, I'll ask Leslie to show you the embalming room when you two return from the hospital."

"The hospital?" I asked.

Leslie walked in as Harold rose. "Greg, meet Leslie. She is studying to be a funeral director and has been with us for five years now."

Leslie was a very beautiful and confident woman with a strong handshake. "Ready?" she asked.

"I think," I said.

"Greg, you and Leslie are going over to Children's Hospital for a pick-up."

I looked over at Leslie and then Harold. "Wow, and here I thought I had been through the worst . . . "

Leslie shook her head. "Honey, the day has barely begun."

Children's Hospital

"Why the unmarked white van?" I asked as we headed out to Children's Hospital.

Leslie paused. "It's unassuming. It doesn't draw attention to itself, and it makes it easy to slide in and slide out without much fanfare."

"That makes sense," I said, before changing the subject. "Tell me something, does what we are about to do impact you in any way?"

"Of course it does," she said, "especially when it comes to children."

"How do you cope with it?"

"I focus on being professional and doing a quality job; that means being there for the families and helping them cope with their loss. But inside," as she pointed to her heart, "I'm feeling their pain. How can I not!"

"So, what is it we are about to do?" I asked.

"We are picking up a premature baby who died from complications last night."

A heaviness came over me, as we pulled into a reserved spot in the back of the hospital.

Leslie put on her game face. "Let's go."

I followed her as we walked through the back entrance, across two corridors, and down a set of stairs; clearly, she had been here before. Waiting for us, as we walked down into the next room, were a couple of nurses with sad expressions on their faces. One had some type of insulated container in her hands and handed it over to me.

My eyes must have doubled in size as I looked over at Leslie for rescue.

She nodded for me to take the container.

I took it and held it tight, like I wanted to protect it. I was holding a baby!

As we drove back toward the funeral home, with the container safely secured on my lap, I thought about the parents of this infant, and the devastation they must be feeling. It made me sad on one hand, and honored on the other. I felt honored to be a part of this life-to-death transition for this baby, this person, this soul.

I looked over at Leslie and said, "I'm beginning to see why this is no ordinary job; why it takes a special person to do this kind of work."

She smiled. "It's why I do it."

"Say more about that?" I asked.

"I feel like I'm doing something that matters. Everybody will experience the loss of a loved one at some point in his or her life, right?"

"Of course."

"Think about it," she said. "I'm in a profession that touches everyone. How many people can say that?"

I couldn't disagree.

She continued: "Whenever I think I have it bad, I think about these families and what they are going through. Things quickly get put back into perspective, if you know what I mean."

Back at the funeral home, we pulled into an area behind the main building that I hadn't seen before.

"What now?" I asked.

"We are going to put the baby's remains into the cooler."

"Wait, the cooler? Is it what I think it is?" I said.

She nodded. "Brace yourself." And just to make sure I knew she was serious, she added, "This might be hard to see," as she pushed opened the heavy door.

The cold temperature was the first thing I noticed as I entered the cooler. Leslie was a few steps ahead of me and placed the container with the deceased baby on a nearby table. I stopped near the door, not knowing if I was supposed to follow or not and looked around. My mouth dropped.

"Are you okay?" she asked, looking concerned.

"I'm not sure," I said, feeling numb.

She nodded to signal that she understood. "This is where we bring the bodies when we first get them. As you can see, they arrive just as they were when they passed."

"I can see that," I said, unable to take my eyes off of the middle-aged woman with a brightly colored dress lying closest to us. "How did she die?"

Leslie shared what she knew about the woman and a few of the others in the room.

I felt so sad as I looked around, knowing full well that each deceased body had been alive within the last 24 hours. Talk about an eerie feeling. I mean, it's one thing to see a deceased body after it's been embalmed, cleaned up, and dressed for presentation. But it's an entirely different thing to see a body still in the throes of death. It was all too real—each body revealing the last few seconds of its life.

Just then another voice startled me from the doorway.

"I'm Jason," he said. "I was asked to show you the embalming room and the crematory."

I look at Leslie for some kind of closure from our time together.

She smiled and made the introductions. "Jason meet Greg. Greg meet Jason."

As Leslie took off, she called back, "I'll catch you later this afternoon. You and I will be setting up a viewing in Lakewood. See you then."

I glanced over at Jason, "A viewing?"

He nodded. "But that's later. Right now, we're headed for the embalming room and the crematory. After that you are on your own for lunch and I believe . . . " as he paused to look at a schedule in his hand, "you'll be working a memorial ceremony after lunch. How does that sound?"

"Sure thing," I said, trying to appear upbeat while still feeling numb.

The embalming room looked like a medical laboratory with four tables evenly spread out. Two of the tables were occupied: one held a teenage boy who was killed the night before in a car accident. He was tall and thin and had long, flowing hair; the kind of guy who would stand out in a crowd and probably be very popular with the ladies.

I shook my head. "It's a shame."

Jason agreed. "I have a son his age. Probably knows him, in fact."

"Do you ever get used to this?" I asked.

"Yes and no. I get used to the tasks at hand. For me it's like a craft. But the stories are always different, and some touch me on a very deep level. Take this guy for example," as he pointed to the teenager. "He was the driver, with three friends in one of those old Volkswagens going down I-25, when an out-of-control car coming from the other direction smashed into them. It wasn't even his fault and now he's gone, and his buddies are in critical condition in the hospital." He shook his head. "That could have been my son."

"I can't even imagine," I said.

Jason stopped to explain the embalming procedure. "What we are doing right now is filling the arteries, veins, and body cavities with antiseptic and preservatives that will delay the decay process."

"Got it!" I said, ready to move on.

He laughed. "A little too much information before lunch?"

I smiled. "You really have to have a sense of humor to be in this industry, don't you?"

"Definitely," he said, as we walked out of the room. "Imagine how difficult it would be if you didn't. People work hard and play hard in this industry. You have to be able to balance out the extremes. When we go to funeral director conferences, we have a great time with our peers. It's a blast."

"I know that," I said. "I've been to those conferences. You're the complete opposite of the stereotype that people have."

"Yeah, that's true. What you have to realize is that, in our industry, it's all about interpersonal skills. We have to be able to connect with families at the most vulnerable time in their lives." He paused before concluding. "We have a wide range of emotions and we have to let those out too, just like everybody else."

The crematory was our last stop before walking outside. Since there was no morning cremation scheduled, I was spared the first-hand experience—for which I was grateful. And although lunch didn't sound all that appealing to me, I definitely needed to take a break. I wanted to see the things I used to take for granted, like the hustle and bustle of normal life. So, I headed out for McDonald's, which was right across the street.

And then things got even more bizarre. I was seeing dead people. That's right, dead people. I know; sounds like I've lost my mind, right? There I was, standing in line to order my food, surrounded by your typical suburbia crowd. They were all very much alive, but instead of seeing life, I was seeing death.

It was so surreal. Instead of seeing a vibrant, middle-aged woman who was in line in front of me, I saw a pale and lifeless woman, lying in waiting. Instead of seeing a smiling teenage girl with rosy cheeks asking for my order, I saw a colorless corpse.

"Can I have your order?"

"What?" I said, trying to get the disturbing images out of my mind. "Do you have anything that's alive?"

"Excuse me?" she said, not understanding the reference.

I smiled and dropped the sarcasm. I knew that if I tried to explain, I would only freak her out.

How can they do this, day in and day out? I thought as I sat down with my meal. The emotional numbness I felt earlier in the day had become heavier now, as I studied the people around me with a new intensity. I was noticing what an eye looks like when it blinks, and how people's lips moved in perfect synchronization with their voices. I saw two guys laughing in line, and how their faces seemed to light up at the exact same moment. Sounds were coming back. Color was returning to people's faces. A surge of energy shot through me. My heart pounded faster.

That's it! I thought, as my mind did a complete 180. *This experience isn't about death at all! It's about life!* By experiencing death all morning, I was developing a greater appreciation for life. But wait—not just for life in general—but specifically for how we live our lives. After all, a corpse is a corpse in the funeral home, whether it had been a multimillionaire, a beauty queen, or a homeless person. What distinguishes each body from the other is what they did with their lives.

Though my insight may seem obvious, it came to me with great clarity. *Appreciate life* was no longer a cliché to me. It really meant something.

Feeling lighter again, I returned to the lobby of the funeral home where I was to meet with Robert, one of the funeral directors. Just then I heard, "Greg, over here."

Robert waved me over to what looked like a line-up. David, the owner and CEO, stood in front of Robert and two other staff members, and inspected their attire. He straightened one person's tie and brushed off a piece of lint from the coat of the other.

David is all about excellence and has been that way as long as I've known him. Every one of his employees is friendly, helpful, attentive, and always dressed immaculately.

Robert introduced me to the team and gave a little background on the memorial service we all were about to work. I remember how appreciative I felt to be considered a member of this team, even if just for the duration of the service.

"What would you like me to do?" I asked, as we all headed toward the chapel on the west side of the building.

Robert handed me a stack of pamphlets for the service. "Why don't you start by handing these out to all the guests at the front entrance."

I nodded, grateful to have a role. Then I saw two men physically holding up a woman who was crying so hard that she couldn't stand by herself. It occurred to me that I was too focused on myself. I needed to remember *why* I was there and *whom* I was serving.

The chapel quickly filled to capacity, and we closed the doors for the start of the service. I have been to many funerals over the years, but never before had I witnessed so much crying and wailing as I saw in that chapel. This man had touched a lot of people on a very deep level.

The service was well-orchestrated by Robert. That I expected. But what I didn't expect was to be so emotionally touched by the service, the family and friends, and the great love in the room. I didn't even know the deceased, but I had so many tears flowing during the eulogies that I had to look away from the people in order to maintain my professionalism.

By the end of the service, I felt like I had lost someone near and dear to me. "Robert," I said, "is this normal?" referring to my bloodshot eyes from crying.

He smiled and put his arm around my shoulder. "Geese, you're just being human!"

"But how do you do it?"

"The tears are there. Just more on the inside than the outside," he said.

The hearse was now waiting by the front entrance.

"Can I watch?"

Robert nodded. "Of course."

Seeing my teammates load the casket into the hearse was bittersweet for me. The last time I had seen this was when my father's body was being loaded into the same vehicle, given that my family also used this funeral home. It was the last time I saw my dad, and that grief reemerged, as if I was reliving that moment again.

"Can I steal you?"

I was relieved to see Leslie. She was smiling. "I've got your next assignment," she said. "We're going out to set up a viewing." She led me back to the familiar white van.

"Is the body already there?"

"No, he's in the back of the van."

"Wait! What?" as I reluctantly turned to look. Sure enough, a large wooden container filled the back of the van.

"Yeah, I thought about FedExing him over, but remembered you wanted the full experience."

"That's a joke, right?" I asked naively, while regaining my composure.

She grinned. "The FedEx part was."

I smiled. "I'm quickly learning how important humor is in your industry, isn't it?"

"Yep. I love to laugh, and some of the people here are a real hoot."

"I totally get why that's important," I added, before changing the subject. "Tell me about this viewing we are about to set up."

She glanced to the back of the van, before introducing me to the mystery passenger who was quietly lying in the box. "The gentleman in the back passed away a couple of days ago and we are headed over to a chapel on the west side of town where his viewing will be held later tonight." She paused for a second and then added, "And I got to work on him."

"What do you mean, 'you got to work on him?'"

"I put him in his favorite suit, did his hair all nice, and touched up his face with a little makeup."

"How did you know what to do?" I asked.

"The family gave me a recent photo to go by. It can be challenging when it's an older photo."

"That's a lot of pressure to try to recreate the essence of a person, isn't it?"

She blushed. "It's what I do."

Moments later we pulled up behind a quaint little chapel in Lakewood. Leslie jumped out and opened a side door of the building, before popping open the back doors of the van.

"What can I do?" I asked.

"Nothing right now," she replied, as she opened up a portable gurney and slid the large box effortlessly on top of it.

I knew from a liability perspective that I wasn't supposed to help out with any moving or lifting, but I felt bad just watching.

Up at the front of the chapel was a pristine, solid oak casket; clearly the Rolls Royce model. It radiated importance!

Like a magician, Leslie lowered the sides of the box and the casket, and slid the body across. It took barely a second.

"Wait, how did you do that?" I asked.

"I can't tell you," she teased. "It's a trade secret."

Up to this point, I had purposely not looked inside the casket. I wasn't sure I wanted to see another dead body. And yet, Leslie was so proud of her work. How could I not at least peek?

I took a deep breath, mustered my confidence, and moved in for a look. I saw a sharply dressed elderly man with a smile of contentment on his face.

"How did you do that?" I asked.

"You mean the smile?"

"Yeah, he looks content."

"Isn't that how you'd want to see all your loved ones look at the end of their life?" she asked.

"Yes, of course," I said. "It really makes a difference."

She nodded. "It says a lot about the value of a smile though, doesn't it?"

Before I could respond, Leslie's cell phone rang. I could tell that it was David, the CEO/owner. Seconds later she hung up and said, "We need to get you back. David wants to meet with you before he leaves for a meeting."

"Are we done here?" I asked.

"For now. Jason will come back tonight to help oversee the viewing."

As we drove back to the funeral home, I noticed how exhausted and emotionally drained I felt.

"Do you ever think about getting out?" I asked.

"Yeah, it's crossed my mind before," she said. "But I'm studying to become a funeral director, and I want to try that out for a while. I think I'd be pretty good with the families."

I nodded, knowing full well that she'd be great with families. "Thank you for today."

Leslie blushed. "I hope it was worth it."

"I am so glad I did this. I had no idea what happens behind the scenes at a funeral home. It was eye opening."

"In a good way I hope," she added.

"Definitely. But it was also a very sobering experience. To be working with life and death in the same moment is not for the lighthearted. You are amazing."

It was late in the afternoon when we pulled into the funeral home parking lot. I gave Leslie a thank you hug and headed toward the lobby where David was waiting.

"Tell me about your day?" he asked, as we headed back to his office.

I walked him through my day.

He said, "That's what you did. Tell me what you learned."

This is why I've always appreciated this man. He is all about authentic communication.

I paused to collect my thoughts. "Can I reflect for a couple of days before sharing with you what I learned? I need to process this whole experience before I can sound intelligent."

He laughed. "Why don't you do that."

After thanking David for the opportunity to work at his funeral home, I headed to my car. I wanted something familiar to bring me back to my reality. But before I could pull out, I saw Harold coming out the front door. He smiled and waved as he headed out to his car. It was the same friendly greeting I got from him eight hours earlier.

Now there's someone who really loves his work, I mused as I pulled away.

What I Learned from My Day at the Funeral Home

- People are uncomfortable talking about death and dying. Ironically, it is the one thing we all have in common and the one thing we will all have to face. It seems to me we should be talking about it more.

- All of the people I had the honor of meeting at the funeral home expressed a higher calling as the reason for choosing this line of work. Being of service to others in a time of need is their passion and purpose. How many professions can you say that about?

- There's customer service and then there's customer service in the funeral industry. *Good* is not acceptable when *great* is the expectation.

- You really need a sense of humor to be working with such life-and-death extremes. It's no wonder people are so funny in this profession.

- Seeing the bodies on the shelves in the preparation room revealed how similar we are all to each other at birth and at death. What's not similar is how we each live our lives.

- By focusing on the needs of the family at hand, funeral home employees are able to stay fully present with their clients, even during the most difficult of difficult times. Try teaching that in a classroom.

- It is reassuring to see the high level of respect and dignity that's demonstrated for each body that is placed in the hands of a funeral home.

- Death is really about the celebration of life.

- We really need to live each day as if it is our last. After seeing the lifeless bodies of a baby and a teenager, it's clear that death can happen to any one of us with a snap of a finger. There are no guarantees.

- Losing a loved one is a memory that will last a lifetime; so too is the experience around their death. Funeral homes play a big part in these lifelong experiences.

- A smile can go a long way.

- There's a lot of pride within this industry, even with the smallest of things, like a shiny casket, a straightened-out tie, well-manicured grounds, or even the smell of potpourri in the CEO's office. Little things become the big things in an industry where everything matters.

- People in the funeral industry deserve a big hug. Talk about unsung heroes! I'm grateful to be affiliated with them!

6
The Chain Reaction

If you think you are too small to be effective, you have never been in a bed with a mosquito.

— Bette Reese

A light blue car stalls in the right lane of a major highway. A backup ensues. It's 6:45 a.m. on Monday.

Within 10 minutes, the stalled car is pushed to the side, sticking out ever so slightly onto the highway.

Within those same 10 minutes, the backup has grown to more than a mile of highway, with no end in sight.

Now cars coming in the other direction begin to slow down, rubber-necking their way past the obstruction.

It's not even 7:00 a.m. yet, and traffic in both directions has come to a near standstill.

The main roads feeding to and from the highway have backed up as well.

Bob, the CFO of a large company downtown, leaves his house in the suburbs and heads toward the highway. Running late already, he needs to make up time. He believes taking the highway will help.

Photo from fotolia by Adobe

Within seconds, he knows that something isn't right. Cars ahead of him are bumper-to-bumper, and he's still a mile away from the highway.

Bob curses his circumstances and pounds the dashboard. He's going to miss a very important meeting, so he picks up his cell phone.

Cheryl, Bob's secretary, wonders why he is being so rude on the phone. She shakes her head after the call, wondering why she puts up with his ranting.

According to Bob's directive, Cheryl has to drop everything she is doing to reschedule his meeting. Contacting seven people and coordinating seven schedules will take up much of her morning, causing her to fall way behind for the day.

Later, Amy waits at a restaurant for her birthday lunch with Cheryl, her best friend. It's 12:10 p.m. and Cheryl is never late.

More time passes and still no Cheryl. Amy, feeling like a loser sitting by herself on her birthday, calls Cheryl to ask where she is. Cheryl, flustered and overwhelmed with work, is short with Amy on the phone. She had completely forgotten Amy's birthday.

After the call, Amy feels distraught and embarrassed, and calls in sick for the remainder of the day. She can't stop thinking about why Cheryl stood her up on her birthday.

That night, Amy can't sleep, tossing and turning.

The next morning, she is completely exhausted from being awake all night. She's a bit depressed as well.

The sun is bright that morning. As Amy floors the gas in order to merge onto the highway, she fails to notice a light blue car sitting on the side of the road, partially in her way. It is the same car that stalled the previous day and had never been removed.

Before she can react, she rear ends the light blue car, causing her own car to slide into oncoming traffic. The first car to hit her flips over, killing the mother, who is driving the car and seriously injuring her four-year-old daughter in the back seat.

Eight more cars crash while trying to avoid the initial accident. This causes a traffic jam that made the previous day's delay seem like a walk in the park.

In the end, there is one fatality and four seriously injured people, including the four-year-old child.

Fortunately, the child recovers. However, she is traumatized over losing her mother and is impacted for the rest of her life.

Lesson

Sometimes we think that what we do doesn't impact others. The truth is, everything we do impacts others in some way, shape, or form.

7

The Day I Became a Pointer Sister

One doesn't discover new lands without consenting to lose sight, for a very long time, of the shore.

— Andre Gide

"You are about to be assigned to a small group. You will be given a task that will require preparation, planning, coordination, and teamwork. You need to complete this task and be ready to go in exactly three hours. Is that clear?"

The crowd of more than 100 participants shouted back, "Yes!"

This was day four of a five-day intensive personal growth workshop out in California. I signed up for this program on the recommendation of a friend who said it changed her life. She highly encouraged me to come check it out; so I did.

The facilitator continued. "Each group will get a unique challenge. Know that the people in your small group are there because you all have something in common."

As the large group of participants began breaking into their assigned smaller groups, I couldn't help wondering who I'd be paired up with and why. I'd been in this workshop for three-and-a-half days and had no idea how I was being perceived by the facilitators. *Surely, I stood out enough to be put in a group of like-minded, successful professionals,* I reasoned as I turned the corner toward the maze of meeting spaces off the hotel lobby.

I glanced to my left where a group of women were gathering and hugging each other like they'd just won an award. I nodded as I passed, admiring their energy. To my right was a coed group forming, laughing, and high-fiving each other like they'd known each other for years.

I hope that's my group, I mused as I headed toward them. Just then a loud shout came from the other side of the hallway.

"Greg, we're over here!"

I looked up and instantly winced to myself, *This must be a mistake!*

Over in the corner were four men, each looking more out-of-place than the other. Frank, the only one I knew, was waving me over.

"You made it!" he said, and proceeded to introduce me to the others. "Greg, this is Paul and that's TJ and Jerron."

We all stood there for a moment, awkwardly staring at each other. I tried my best to mask my disappointment. You see, these men did have something in common. They were the quiet guys in the workshop who never actively participated or spoke up. *So why am I in this group?* I lamented quietly. *These guys are losers! I just don't see the connection!*

Now, granted, my initial assessment of the group wasn't fair. I didn't know these men. And the only reason I knew Frank was because we briefly chatted in the lobby the first morning. I needed to try to make this work. After all, there had to be a reason we were together—even if it didn't make sense to me at the time.

"Now that we are all here, I'll go ahead and read our stretch assignment," said Paul.

"Stretch Assignment? This should be interesting," I said. We all braced ourselves.

Paul began, *"The following assignment is unique to your group and tailored for the individuals in it. You have exactly three hours to do the following:*

1. *You are to become the Pointer Sisters.*
2. *You are to dress and look like the Pointer Sisters.*
3. *You must be prepared to sing their song, "I'm So Excited!"*
4. *The song must be sung in a cappella.*
5. *You will perform the song in front of all the participants.*

"Is this a joke?" asked TJ. He looked like he had just woken up from a bad dream.

"And who the hell are the Pointer Sisters?" added Frank.

I jumped in on the whining. "And what do they mean by a cappella? I'm hoping it means the *short* version of the song?"

Paul shook his head. "Dude, it means we have to sing without music." The rest of us looked at each other in shock. "In other words," he continued, "we're screwed!"

By this point, most of the other groups had already dashed out of the hotel as if they were contestants in *The Amazing Race*.

"Let's get to the mall," shouted Jerron. "We need dresses. We'll go in my van."

"Wait, what . . . ," I cried, "we're buying dresses?" The men ignored me and took off toward the parking lot. I went after them.

Jerron looked like he was a member of the ZZ Top band with his long beard and matching ponytail. And his dilapidated van only added to the mystique. But it was definitely the slight stench of marijuana coming from the inside that made me feel like I was an extra in a Cheech and Chong movie.

"Got any munchies?" I joked as we sped off. No response.

After frantically searching his iPhone, Frank shouted, "Here they are."

"Who?" asked Paul.

"The Pointer Sisters performing on YouTube," replied Frank. He passed the phone around. "Brace yourselves."

As we took turns watching, the van became uncomfortably quiet. Finally, TJ spoke: "We're in big trouble!"

We all broke out laughing, realizing the absurdity of this assignment.

"Guys, guys! Here's what we'll do," suggested Paul. "Let's just get in, grab some dresses, and get out. We'll figure the rest out later."

"Again with the dresses," I teased, as the laughter morphed into discomfort and fear.

"Are we really going to do this?" stammered Jerron, as we pulled into Orange County's version of the Mall of America.

"I don't think we have a choice," replied Paul. "Let's just do it!"

Without hesitation, we all jumped out of the van and took off running—but in different directions. No conversation, no plan, no nothing. It was the oddest thing. *So much for the bonding experience,* I mumbled. I followed Frank, the slowest one.

Time was becoming a factor as more and more panic set in. Frank and I ran toward the mall directory when my cell phone rang. "Greg, it's Paul. Come over to the Super Kmart. They have cheap dresses here."

I grabbed Frank and we hustled over as quickly as we could, dodging people left and right on our way. Within minutes, we were reunited in the women's clothing aisle in Super K, pulling cheap dresses off the rack.

"Where's TJ?" shouted Paul.

"Oh no!" cried Frank as he spotted TJ coming out of the next aisle, waiving a handful of wigs in the air.

"Guys, I got the last five wigs from the Halloween aisle."

"And I found some lipstick and eyeliner," added Jerron.

I could only shake my head. *What have I gotten myself into?*

"We'll dress in the van," screamed Paul, directing us toward the cashiers.

I looked at my watch. "We're down to 75 minutes."

We sprinted to the van and piled in for the second time. Frank then pulled out his iPhone where he had downloaded our song, "I'm So Excited," and began playing it as we sped back to the hotel.

"Luckily there aren't a lot of words," I said, trying to cheer myself up.

As we approached the hotel parking lot, we could see all the other groups from the program spread out across the lot practicing dance moves to music. The scene could have passed for *American Idol* tryouts as each group worked on their choreography.

"At least we're all doing the same thing," said Paul, clearly feeling a little relieved.

"Yeah, maybe five white guys imitating three black women won't stand out as much," sarcastically added Frank.

With time running out, we finished dressing in the back of the van while attempting to apply eyeliner and lipstick. Then we set up our own minidance studio in our corner of the parking lot, using Jerron's van to block us from the other groups.

"Now what?" pleaded TJ.

"We . . . dance . . . I guess?" replied Frank.

"No one said anything about dancing," said Paul. "I think we just sing the song."

"I know. Let's stand together in a line and clap our hands to the song as we sing," I suggested. "Besides, we don't have time to put a dance together anyway."

Just then a loud horn sounded from the hotel. Our time was up. We would have to improvise.

"But we're not even close to being ready," cried Jerron. "Maybe they'll give us more time?"

"It's too late, buddy," said Paul. "We just need to do this."

My heart was pounding as we walked toward the main entrance. We were wearing Kmart dresses and cheap Halloween wigs with poorly done makeup on our faces. But it didn't matter. I knew enough about these moments to know that Paul was right; we just needed to do it. This was about the experience; not whether or not we looked like or sounded like the Pointer Sisters.

The large ballroom was buzzing as each group nervously awaited the start of the show. Suddenly the lights dimmed, and a big spotlight appeared in the center of the room. The buzzing quieted to a low murmur, and an amplified voice took control.

"And now I'd like to introduce our first performance of the evening. Singing a cappella, please welcome the Pointer Sisters!"

The crowd went crazy as the five of us made our way to the front of the room. We lined up together, as planned, while the first part of the song played over the loudspeakers to help get us started. Right away we began clapping and bellowing out the chorus. Then the music faded, leaving our off-key voices without accompaniment.

Now I have to be honest here and say my memory of what transpired next is a little foggy.

I remember that we broke off in five different directions (surprise, surprise) while belting out the words, "I'm so excited," over and over and over again. Clearly none of us could recall any of the other words to the song. I also remember going into the audience and kissing as many people on the cheek as I could find. And although I have no idea why I did that or what it had to do with the song, it did help fill the awkwardness of a song that never seemed to end.

But we did it! And when our song was over, all the other participants swarmed in and lifted each of us up in the air, as if we had just scored the winning goal in the World Cup finals. I must admit, I've never felt that level of exhilaration in my life before (or since) as I did right then.

The rest of the evening followed the same format. Each group performed and got to experience the exhilaration of being lifted in the air.

Reflections

As part of our completion activities the next day, we were asked to reconvene into our small groups to debrief the previous day's experience. The discussion in our group went something like this:

Paul: That was fun. More fun than I ever would have expected.

Me: The fun for me didn't kick in until the song was pretty much over and I knew we were done.

TJ: I was pretty much uncomfortable the whole time.

Paul: Why?

TJ: That's not how I like to have fun. But that's just me.

Jerron: I had a blast. And I appreciate getting to know you guys.

Frank: Like Greg, I too was uncomfortable, but started to enjoy it toward the end. Being lifted up by everyone was pretty cool.

Me: So, what did we learn?

Paul: Regardless of the different levels of anxiety that activity raised in each of us, we still came together and succeeded. For that we should be proud of ourselves.

Frank: Agreed.

Jerron: I realize the tight time frame was part of the test to see how we'd do under pressure. I would have preferred spending some time getting to know each other. That part was missing for me.

Me: Me too. Without that relationship piece, I didn't feel as connected to you guys. We could have been a stronger team with a deeper connection. And to be honest, getting through that experience felt more like an individual accomplishment than a team accomplishment for me.

TJ: Good point. It was more of an individual victory for me as well.

Paul: So, you're saying relationships matter in teams.

Frank: Yes. We were successful around the task but not as successful around the relationship aspect. Had we also taken the time to bond a little, imagine how amazing that ending would have felt!

Me: What's our takeaway from this?

Jerron: There needs to be a balance between the task and the relationships in order to be successful.

Paul: Amen, brother! And can I say one more thing?

Jerron: Please.

Paul: You guys are the ugliest chicks I've ever seen!

8
Like Hell You Will!

> What do we live for if not to make the
> world less difficult for each other.
>
> — George Eliot

was student body president at Western State
College in Gunnison, Colorado. One of the
many perks that came with the job was a trip out to the Coors
Brewery in Golden for a special tour given to all the student body
presidents from the various colleges and universities across the
state. They flew us all in.

In truth, the real reason for this gathering was for the brewery
to promote their college marketing department and to encourage
each of us to consider Coors for future promotional and sponsorship
opportunities on our individual campuses. Interestingly, much of
the persuasion came while we were testing the various brands
of complimentary beer. Perhaps that's why I left Golden fully committed to the brand, even though I couldn't see that at the time.
Nevertheless, it was a fun trip, and I got to meet many of the key
marketing execs from Coors while there.

As graduation approached, my future was still up in the air. I had applied to Miami University (of Ohio) for graduate school that included an assistantship, but hadn't heard anything. The assistantship would pay my tuition, room and board, and provide a modest stipend each month. Without it, I couldn't afford to go, so it was an all-or-nothing deal for me.

And then I got the phone call. "Greg, this is Jason Dawl from college marketing over at Coors. We have a position opening up in our department and I want to encourage you to apply for it."

"Me? Really?" I asked, in a complete state of shock.

"Yes. Our reps have really enjoyed working with you at the college and thought you'd be a great addition to the team here."

"Tell me more," I asked, trying to hide my enthusiasm.

"You'd be on a team of Coors liaisons with colleges and universities across the country. You'd help us sponsor events and create branding with Coors on the campuses. It would involve a lot of traveling, hanging out with college students, and having a lot of fun." He was teasing me now. "Are you interested?"

I tried my hardest to sound like I had hundreds of offers on the table already. "I'll definitely look into it." Of course, what I really wanted to say was, *Are you kidding me! I'd do that for free!*

Two days later, with Coors still on my mind, I received a thick packet in the mail from Miami University. Well aware that getting a packet that big could only be good news, I frantically opened it up and pulled out the cover letter. It read,

> *Dear Greg, we'd like to congratulate you on your acceptance into the graduate school. You've also been granted a full assistantship in residential life and will receive out-of-state tuition, room and board, and a monthly stipend. Welcome to Miami.*

I nearly jumped out of my shoes, that is, until I spotted an empty Coors can on my counter from the graduation party the night before.

Oh wait, I realized, *things could very easily get complicated here. What if Coors were to offer me a job? What would I do then?*

Whenever I'm ambivalent about something, I can usually count on my father for guidance. I called him immediately to share the news.

"That's great, son. I'm so proud of you." And then just before hanging up he added, "I'm sure you'll make the right decision. We'll see you when you get home."

I thanked him for his support and hung up, wondering what he meant by *the right decision?*

Shortly after graduation I moved back home with my parents and took the interview with Coors. *Why not,* I figured, *it's always good to have options.*

Two days later Jason called with the offer. "Are you ready to come work for Coors? We'd like to offer you a position with college marketing."

"Are you serious! This is one of the best days of my life!" I said, as my stomach tightened into knots. As excited as I was to get the offer, not getting it would have made my life a lot easier. Now I had to make a decision that I wasn't ready or prepared to make. "Can I think about it and call you tomorrow?"

"Of course, you can. I'll be sitting by the phone," he said, trying to be funny.

I hung up with my heart pounding out of control. *Crap, what am I going to do? I want to do both.*

As evening approached, I contacted a couple buddies and asked them out for a drink to help me make this all-important decision. Three rounds later, I came to what seemed to be an obvious conclusion, possibly influenced by the fact that we were drinking Coors beer. Now all I had to do was convince my father.

As I drove home, I thought about previous career conversations with my dad. *He's always given me grief for choosing psychology over business as a major,* I argued. He'd say over and over again, "There's no jobs in psychology. You can't go wrong with a business degree."

I knew he was probably right about all of that, but I went the psychology route anyway. And I'd be lying if I said it didn't create a little bit of tension between us.

That's it! I thought as I got off the exit near the house, *I'll emphasize to him that I did take his advice after all and went with the business option. He'll be thrilled. Besides, he's a marketing and advertising guy himself; why wouldn't he want me to follow in his footsteps?*

As I drove up the driveway, I could see a light was still on in the den. It was about 1:00 a.m. and my parents were always in bed by 9:00 p.m. *Why would a light be on in the den?* I thought as I got out of the car and approached the front door. I recalled the many nights sneaking back into the house late at night when I was in high school. I eased the door open and tiptoed toward the stairs.

A faint voice jetted out from across the room. "Is that you?"

I saw my father sitting in the recliner by the light. "Yes, it's me," I whispered, "what are you still doing up?"

"I couldn't sleep," he said, "and I wanted to know what you decided."

"About what?" I asked, trying to downplay the moment.

"About graduate school."

"Oh, that," as I looked away for a second, trying to gather up some confidence for what I was about to say next. "You'll be happy to know that I decided to go with Coors."

His eyes pierced right through me. "The hell you will!"

"What?" I exclaimed, hoping he didn't just say what I thought he said.

"You heard me," he replied. "If you go with Coors, I'll disown you from this family."

First an outright disagreement, now a threat! It felt like I had just been sucker punched in the stomach. "You'll what? Why? I don't get this. Why are you so upset? I thought you'd be happy that I picked Coors. Besides," I pleaded, "it's a marketing position. You of all people should appreciate that."

My father raised his hand to change the tempo of the conversation. His face softened as he invited me to sit down.

"Look," he said, "there's something I need to tell you that has been bothering me for years."

Oh great, I wondered, *is this where he tells me how much I've disappointed him?*

He took a deep breath before speaking. "I never finished college. I don't have a degree. It's been one of the biggest regrets I've ever had."

Somewhat relieved that his secret wasn't about me, I leaned in. "But you went to St. Thomas College. I just assumed you graduated."

There was an uncomfortable silence. I could see that he was really embarrassed about this. "Dad, you are the president of one of the top advertising agencies in Colorado. Before that you were vice president at Leo Burnett, one of the top advertising agencies in the world. You made United Airlines commercials that won national awards! What does it matter if you had a degree or not—you reached the pinnacle of your profession!"

He shook his head in disagreement. "All my peers have MBAs; some even have doctorate degrees. I've never felt like I was on the same level with them."

Before I could respond, he straightened up and looked me right in the eyes, like only a father can do. "You now have the opportunity to get a master's degree—for free no less! Can't you see how valuable this once-in-a-lifetime opportunity is? I don't care if you get a degree in *dodgeball*, it's still a master's degree and no one can ever take that away from you."

They give out master's degrees in dodgeball? I thought before his absurd point sunk in. "So, this whole conversation isn't about Coors but about the value of an education?" I asked.

"That's right," he said. "Jobs come and go, but having a master's degree says something about you as a person. It reveals your character, commitment, and discipline. It's more than a piece of paper."

My father had made a compelling argument. I realized in that moment that getting a master's degree would not be just for me but for him as well.

"Alright," I conceded, "I'll go graduate school."

As I stood up, I was caught off guard by a flood of emotions. I felt a connection to my father that I'd never felt before. Our relationship had transformed from the all-too-familiar father-son connection into a true friendship; something I had always yearned for with him. We embraced as friends for the first time in my adult life.

Afterthoughts

I graduated from Miami University with my master's degree in the spring of 1982. Without question, going back to school was the right decision. Ironically, Coors eliminated the college marketing department a couple of years after they had offered the job to me.

My father and I never talked about what happened that night again. When I referred to it in a toast I gave him on his 80th birthday, he smiled and nodded, letting me know that he remembered.

Since his passing a few years ago, I reflect back to that night with bittersweet feelings. Although a monumental turn in our relationship, I am still bothered by the fact that my father felt such a void in his life for not having finished college. He was one of the most successful men I've ever known, and yet, he couldn't see it himself. Sure, a college degree, or an advanced degree, is important in today's world, but it shouldn't define who we are.

John Giesen was a loving husband and father who, together with my mother, raised six kids, each one successful in their own right. He cared about people and made a difference in the lives of everyone he came into contact with. His legacy will always be about who he was, not what he had.

May you rest in peace, Dad!

9
I Thought I Knew Tony

In the end, we only regret the chances we didn't take.

— Lewis Carroll

"You've been Tony's friend for a long time. Will you get up and say something at his memorial service?" asked Susan, Tony's wife. Her sad and desperate eyes left no room for me to decline.

"Of course," I said, feeling both honored and apprehensive. Tony was a great guy and all, but our conversations over the years had been pretty superficial. You know, guy stuff. We'd open with weather, move to sports, and end on women. He particularly liked listening to my dating stories, as most of my married friends did. Our most meaningful conversations were the few occasions when Tony shared his struggles in his marriage. Not exactly eulogy material.

In fairness, I made a point to spend time with Tony during his year-long battle with cancer; the disease that has taken a handful of my friends from this life. But instead of talking about his cancer and how he was feeling about it, I focused on more positive topics in an attempt to cheer him up. At least, that was my rationale at the time. I feel differently now.

With little time to prepare for Tony's memorial, I needed first to figure out what to say. Surely, I had a funny story, an embarrassing moment, or a profound memory of some sort . . . didn't I?

Hours went by and nothing.

I called mutual friends. Still nothing.

I wondered: *How can I know him for so many years and yet at the same time not know him at all?*

The Back-Up Plan

Time was up, though the best story I had wouldn't come to me until months later. I had to go with my lame back-up plan for Tony's eulogy. I would recite one of my favorite readings, *Bits and Pieces*. It's a powerful piece about all the different people who come into our lives and the impact that they leave on us. Ironic, right?

The service was intimate, and packed. Between Tony and his wife, they had many friends. And yet, only two of us got up to say a few words. The guy before me shared a couple memories and concluded by ripping off his shirt. He revealed a sleeveless undershirt, similar to the style we associated with Tony. It was a clever ending. Then I got up and gave my reading.

The service ended. We ate cake. People mingled. Some thanked me for the nice words.

I was sad and disappointed.

I knew why I was sad, but I couldn't tell with whom I was more disappointed—myself for my lame eulogy or Tony for not being more interesting. *Why didn't he give me more material to work with?*

And then it hit me a couple months later.

The real story I should have shared wasn't about Tony at all. It was about me. That's right, me. I failed to take our friendship to the next level. I could have asked him how he was feeling. I could have asked him to describe what it was like to be told you only have three months to live. I could have asked him if he had any regrets. But I didn't do any of that. I missed out on an incredible opportunity.

The truth is, I was uncomfortable talking about his cancer. And because our previous conversations had lacked substance, it felt awkward to change the communication paradigm between us—even though cancer already had done that.

I don't know about you, but I hope that when my time comes, my friends, family, and colleagues have plenty to say about me, our relationships, and the impact I had on their lives. I don't want them to draw a blank with nothing to say. That would mean we all had failed.

So, if you are called on to say a few words at my memorial, may I make a request? Please don't bring anything to read. No poems. No verses. Nada. Instead, I want to hear how I've touched you. I want to hear your favorite memory of us and why it mattered. I want to know how our relationship made you a better person.

I hope that isn't asking too much.

10
What's a Man Walk?

People may forget what you have said, and they
may forget what you have done, but they will
never forget how you made them feel.

— Teresa Spangler

"You should join us Wednesday night," my friend Coy said to me as we were finishing up our breakfast meeting.

"What's Wednesday night?" I asked curiously.

"A bunch of guys meet up at Washington Park every Wednesday evening and we walk around the park." Then he paused for a second. "Actually, we do more than that."

I couldn't let that last comment go. "What do you mean you do more than that?"

Coy straightened up and looked me right in the eyes. "I mean, it's not as much about the walk as it is about what transpires during the walk. We call it the *Man Walk*. It is about men getting together to bond, share their feelings, and support each other. It's powerful. You have to experience it for yourself."

"Really! How many guys participate?" I asked.

"It varies—anywhere from 6 to 12 men. Most live near the park and walk over."

"So, tell me more about these men?"

"They're doctors, lawyers, and businessmen like us. Most are married and have families." And then his voice softened. "These men are unique. They are drawn to the brotherhood that this group provides. They want to open up to other men and share their struggles without fear of being judged."

I was getting more and more interested. "Like what kind of struggles?"

Coy was getting animated now as he rattled off examples. "The struggle of being a husband, a father, or a son. The struggle of traveling so much that you become disconnected from your own family. The struggle of having to be the primary bread winner and the pressure that goes with that. The struggle of being in a bad marriage. The struggle of having to find a nursing home for your mother, who would rather die than be put into such a place."

Then he smiled at me. "You know, the kind of issues that men don't often share with each other."

I nodded. "You had me at husband—father—son."

He laughed. "Great. We'll see you on Wednesday?"

I smiled. "I need to see what this man walk is all about. I'll be there."

Now I'll be honest, as Wednesday approached, I found myself looking for reasons not to go. Plus, I've been in a "men's group" before and wasn't really interested in joining another one. But despite my resistance, I ended up going anyway and am glad I did. What an amazing experience it was, and with some amazing guys.

Wednesday Night

The evening began at Coy's house. I strolled in at around 7:45 p.m. and we spent some time catching up before heading over to the park, by way of Dave's house. Since most of the guys lived in the area, it wasn't unusual to stop at each other's houses along the way. Dave was one of the founding members of the group and probably the most instrumental in making it work. His garage, better known as the Swamp, was the man cave for many of the guys in the neighborhood. It was decorated in Grateful Dead memorabilia, complete with couches, a TV, and a refrigerator. It was too cool!

I asked Coy and Dave to talk a little about the concept of the man walk before heading out. Dave began by telling me how much this group of men have meant to him. "This is more than friendship," he said, "This is brotherhood. We love each other."

"And we're truly there for each other," added Coy. "It's been a blessing to be a part of this band of brothers."

It was 9:00 p.m. by the time we reached Washington Park. The temperature was about 50 degrees and there was a full moon shining overhead. Suddenly, as if on command, men approached us from all directions. Clearly these men all know each other, evident by the loud greetings, laughter, and hugging.

This must be the group, I whispered awkwardly; like I was looking in from the outside.

"Let's circle up," yells Dave. Within seconds the 12 men formed a circle for their ritual check-in. Then, one by one, each man shared a little about what was going on with him. Some shared very vulnerable things, while others kept it to how they were feeling in the moment. I was so touched by the level of openness and honesty they displayed. It made me want to open up to them as well. But the best part for me was how each man ended with the words, "I'm in." To me that meant, "I'm here and I'm committed to being a part of this group."

After check-in, we set off for our 2.5 mile walk around the park. Some men walked in small groups while others paired up (with the configuration always changing). The topics of conversations also varied. At one moment I was talking about my job while at another moment I shared the legacy I hope to leave on earth. There were no boundaries—anything was fair game.

Near the middle of the walk, Dave asked the whole group to circle up again. This time he asked Britt to step into the middle of the circle. Britt was about to leave town for three months and Dave wanted to give him a formal send-off. Then, one-by-one, each man gave a comment, or a blessing, or simply a hug to say goodbye to him. Again, I was blown away. *Who are these guys?*

At about 10:00 pm we completed our walk and we circled up one last time for the check-out. As with the check-in, each man got a chance to say something to the group. This time, everyone ended with the words, "I'm out."

When the band of brothers dispersed, it was as they began—with loud goodbyes, laughter, and lots of hugging.

Final Thoughts

The walk itself took maybe an hour, but the memory for me will last a lifetime. I wish I could have gathered with these men on a weekly basis, but I taught graduate school on Wednesday nights at that time, making it virtually impossible to attend on a regular basis. That was my loss.

Men need men—not just for sports or a slap on the back—but for support, brutal honesty, and brotherhood. We need a safe place to be vulnerable without judgment, comparison, or competition. We need these man walks.

Thank you Coy and Dave for creating this band of brothers. I look forward to coming back to the group, especially now that I live in the hood.

I'm Greg Giesen and I'm Out!

11
I'll Go Fifth!

Life begins at the end of your comfort zone.

— Neale Donald Walsch

Early in my career, I was a management trainer for a Denver-based employers' council, teaching more than 20 different leadership and soft-skill courses for client companies across the country. I was pretty good too. My repeat business was at an all-time high as my clients continually asked me back. By most people's standards, I was very successful.

And yet something was missing.

My trainings were starting to blend together, causing me to sound more robotic in the process. I found myself in a rut, simply going through the motions without the passion that always went hand-in-hand with my words. My energy was fading; I was burning out.

Right about this time, I overheard a conversation in the break room between a couple of my colleagues, Terry and Sara, about an adventure program that Terry had done on a high ropes course.

I couldn't resist interrupting, "What's a high ropes course?" I asked.

Terry smiled, happy to draw me in. "A high ropes course involves a series of challenging activities high off the ground," as he pointed up toward the ceiling. "Picture a telephone pole and you have an idea about how high off the ground I'm talking about."

"And what's the point of these activities?" I asked.

"You almost have to experience it for yourself to truly understand the value. What I can tell you is that you'll learn more about yourself than you'd ever imagine."

As Terry continued talking about his high ropes experience, my mind drifted over to my own dilemma. I interrupted him again. "Do you think that program would help me do a reset on life?" I was only half joking.

He nodded. "And a whole lot more! You should do it."

I realized that this was exactly what I needed. "Then I'm doing it!"

I felt a surge of energy—something I hadn't felt for quite a while. I walked to my office and registered for the next program before I could talk myself out of it.

The High Ropes Course

After few, light, team-building exercises to start the morning off, our instructor Tim pointed over to our next activity, off in the distance. We all gazed in the direction of his finger.

About 50 yards away was the infamous Power Pole, a 35-foot pole with a small platform on top. I winced, *Are you kidding me!*

Fortunately, or unfortunately, I had seen this activity on YouTube before. First you have to climb to the top of the pole with nothing but a belay rope. Then you have to maneuver yourself up on the platform so you can stand on top of the pole. And if that's not enough, the pole wobbles and the only way down is to jump and trust that your teammates are still holding on to the belay rope to let you down.

Simple enough, right?

Not if you have a fear of heights, or trust issues, or balance problems, or any other limitation—whether physical, emotional, or mental. In fact, the woman who was climbing the pole on the YouTube video began hyperventilating as she reached the top and literally froze. Eventually a rescue team had to peel her off the pole and help her back down.

But that was about her. This will be nothing like that, I wanted to believe.

As we approached, the pole appeared taller and thinner. I panicked. *I'm not sure I can do this! That thing doesn't look sturdy. What if I start hyperventilating like that lady did in the video? And why are we doing the power pole right off the bat? Shouldn't we ease into something this dangerous?*

I sized up the other nine participants in the program. I needed a strategy. I needed a plan . . . a survival plan.

And then it came to me. *I know, I'll go fifth!*

It was the perfect plan. I'd place myself right smack in the middle of the group, thereby enabling me to carefully watch and learn from the first four! By the time my turn came, I'd know exactly what to do. I giggled thinking that going in the middle also would separate me from the few more fearful stragglers than me who undoubtedly would get stuck on the pole like the lady in the video.

With my strategy intact, I was ready.

Or so I thought.

At the base of the pole, Tim asked us all to sit down. He grabbed a nearby stick and drew a circle in the dirt.

"Do you see this circle? This circle represents your comfort zone. The inside is where your greatest comfort comes from; it's what you know . . . it's what you're used to . . . and it's safe."

Then he pointed to the area outside the circle. "What do you think this area represents?"

"Risk," shouted one participant.

"The unknown," added another.

"Our growth area," I yelled, still not sure where he was going with the demonstration.

Tim smiled. "That's right. So, what's our natural tendency when we get to the edge of our comfort zone? Do we take a step out or do take a step back in?"

We all looked at each other before someone said, "I think we move back into the comfort zone."

Tim nodded. "I think you're right. And here's the problem with that. Imagine that each time we retreat back into the comfort zone, we add a layer of bricks around the outside of the circle . . . and then another layer and another layer. Eventually the bricks get so high that we can no longer see out."

"So, what you are saying," I added, "is that instead of our comfort zone expanding, it closes in and gets smaller."

Tim's eyebrows lifted up. "Yes!"

"But how do you know if that's happening?" asks another participant.

"Simple. You stop taking risks. You stop challenging yourself." And then he paused before emphasizing, "You stop growing."

At this point we were all so focused on the conversation, that we forgot about the giant power pole looming in front of us.

Tim pointed to the edge of the circle again. "Tell me this. What would happen to our circle, our comfort zone, if instead of retreating we took a baby step outside the circle?"

"Your circle expands!" someone shouted.

"Exactly," Tim said. "And this power pole activity is an opportunity for many of you to expand your comfort zones."

It was as if I had been hit by one of those metaphoric bricks. *Ah! Now I see where he's going with all of this. He was talking about me!* I realized that I was living in a shrinking comfort zone. No wonder I had lost my passion, I couldn't see over the brick wall that was blocking my view. And to top it off, my "I'll go fifth" strategy was more of the same.

I was reminded of the quote, "If you want things to stay the same, then keep doing what you are doing," which was what I was doing. I thought more about it. *Why did I sign up for this workshop in the first place? Wasn't it to shake things up in my life and discover what's important? Or, was it to continue doing what I always do, and thus get the results I always get?*

The answer was clear to me. I put myself in this workshop so I could change things up and view the world from a different perspective. Maintaining the status quo was no longer acceptable. And that meant, "going fifth" was no longer an option. It was time for a bold move!

Tim's voice suddenly brought me back to the group. "So, who wants to go first?"

I cringed and raised my hand. I felt like I was back in second grade, hoping someone else would get picked. But no, not this time. Instead, everyone in the group looked over at me and shouted, with conviction, "Yes! Geese needs to go first!"

All I could think was, *Crap! Was it that obvious?*

The Power Pole

If I thought too much about what I was doing, it would be the kiss of death. I raced up the pole, making sure to not look down. At the top I was faced with the difficult challenge of lifting myself up to the loose platform that sits on top of the pole. This was much more difficult than I could have ever imagined. Not only was there nothing to hold on to, but I suddenly remembered that I was 35 feet above ground, hanging on to a pole that was swaying in the wind.

It was a moment that I'll never forget. Part of me wanted to hold on for dear life, hoping to wake up from this nightmare with the realization that it was only a dream, while the other part of me wanted to persevere, trusting that I'd find a way to triumph.

The voices from the group grew louder. "Come on, Geese, you can do it! You're almost there!"

I heard every comment and suggestion. In fact, I totally relied on the group to slowly and methodically instruct me the rest of the way. "Now move your left hand to the other side . . . that's right, just like that. Excellent! Now place both feet together and gently lift . . . nice and slow."

Before I knew it, I was standing on the little platform on top of the pole. My body was literally trembling from head to toe, but it didn't matter. I had done it. I made it to the top! The group cheered, "You're the man! You go Geese!"

I tried to smile, but I knew the hardest part still separated me from landing safely back on the ground. I had to leap toward the trapeze that was seven feet away, and grab ahold of it. Again, the group roared from below, "We got you Geese, let her rip!"

I bent my knees just a bit, took a big breath, and lunged like I had never lunged before . . . and totally missed the bar. But you know what? It didn't matter. My team pulled the rope tight at that very moment, causing me to gently sway back and forth as they lowered me to the ground, cheering as they did so.

In that moment, I was emotionally wiped out—yet happily content—like I had just crossed the finish line in a marathon. More importantly, I knew that I had gotten exactly what I was hoping to get from the workshop. I had rediscovered my passion for life! I realized that I had gotten too content with the status quo and my comfort zone was closing in instead of expanding.

I don't remember a whole lot more about the rest of the program, other than I couldn't stop smiling for the whole two days. It was like my inner child had taken over and I could simply play and be a kid again.

Although I continued to have very profound insights about my experience on the pole, I'd like to share a few bullet points of what I learned from that experience:

- The pole itself wasn't that difficult to climb. What made it difficult was how I built the whole experience up in my mind before ever climbing it.

- It is very comfortable to live in my comfort zone, but I stop growing when I do that.

- The easiest way to step out of my comfort zone is by having a goal or desire or outcome that sits just beyond it. However, this requires knowing what I want.

- I had lost my passion back at work because I had lost sight of my purpose. That's what caused my burnout.

- I used to make fun of "purpose statements" but I learned that having a purpose is what gives me direction. And by having a direction, I'm able to know what I want and how to make it happen.

- I never could have successfully climbed the pole without the help from the group below. Likewise, I cannot achieve my purpose in life without the help of others.

- Years later, whenever I'm tempted to "go fifth" in life, I visualize being back on the pole and remind myself that the only thing that separates me from achieving the life I want is me. And if I want something badly enough, all I have to do is go for it with everything I have. That way, even if I miss the trapeze, I will still have expanded my comfort zone.

12

The Tale of Two Women

When one door of happiness closes, another opens;
but often we look so long at the closed door that
we do not see the one which has opened for us.

— Helen Keller

I was 32 years old and driving home from work when I got a frantic phone call. It was from one of my high school friends that I hadn't seen or talked to for more than 16 years.

"Geese, do you have the TV on?"

Startled, I recognized the voice. "Is this Michael Kelly? How the heck are you?"

"I'm fine, man. Are you near a TV?"

Confused, I replied, "I'm pulling into my home right now—and why do I need a TV?"

"Your high school girlfriend is all over the news. Turn on any channel!"

It was May 20, 1988, 13 years since we graduated from high school. I couldn't imagine what girlfriend he was referring to, let alone why she would be on the news. "What are you talking about?"

"Laurie Wasserman shot up a school. I kid you not. She is holding a family hostage and it's all over the news!"

My heart started pounding like I was about to have a heart attack. I ran to the TV in the living room and turned it on, still in a state of shock. Sure enough, news crews had surrounded the outskirts of a large home in Winnetka, Illinois. Hundreds of police and SWAT crews were assembled around the house. News helicopters swarmed overhead. It was as intense a crime scene as you could imagine.

From what I could gather, the police were trying to coax Laurie out of the house. While that was going on, the news crews recounted the day's events:

- Laurie Dann (Wasserman) left her home that morning with three loaded guns and multiple packages of cookies tainted with lead and arsenic.

- She delivered the cookies to two Northwestern University fraternities, babysitting clients, her psychiatrist, and her ex-husband.

- She then went over to another babysitting client and asked the mother if she could take the two kids out for a quick snack. Permission was granted and with the two children in tow, Laurie drove to Ravinia Elementary School, where she started a small fire inside the school.

- From there she hopped over to the Young Men's Jewish Council where, although prevented from entering, she managed to leave a Mickey Mouse cup laced with poisonous juice.

- She then returned to the home of the two children and took them both down to the basement where she set the basement stairway afire and fled.

- At Hubbard Woods School, she held up a classroom, shot and killed 8-year-old Nicholas Corwin, and wounded five other children.

- After fleeing the school, she raced down a private drive where she crashed her car and took off running. She entered the closest house, and is currently holding a family hostage.

- When first entering the house, she shot and wounded Philip Andrew, a college student home for the summer who tried to take her gun away.

I was dumbfounded and glued to the TV. Other former high school friends called to express their horror at what was going on. It was so surreal to be watching all these famous TV news journalists focusing on my hometown and my former high school girlfriend. I just couldn't believe what was happening—and I couldn't help wondering how it was going to end.

At some point, police heard a loud bang from the upstairs bedroom. It created a lot of commotion on the ground, but the police stood down. About an hour later, the SWAT teams entered the house, and found Laurie dead from a self-inflicted gunshot to the head. The all-day nightmare had finally come to an end.

Laurie Wasserman

You've heard of or read "The Tale of Two Cities." How about the "tale of two women?"

The Laurie Wasserman I knew in high school was a far cry from the Laurie Dann that committed the atrocities on May 20, 1988. We became friends our junior year of high school and I found her to be easy going, sensitive, fun, and adventurous. I recall many of my friends giving me grief when our friendship morphed into dating toward the end of that year, not because we were together, but because she was way out of my league. Laurie was extremely attractive and wore clothes that accentuated her figure like no one else could. I, on the other hand, fell more into the nerdy, wannabe-cool category, complete with pimples and a ton of insecurity. And yet, she was as drawn to me as I was to her. We used to spend hours sitting on the back stairs at the high school talking about everything from the meaning of life to our favorite books and TV shows. We had a connection that I didn't have with most women at that age. It was special.

We dated for a little while and went to junior prom together. My favorite memory with Laurie was our last time together at the end of our junior year. We both had ridden our bikes that day and decided to play hooky together near the train tracks. Laurie had stolen a couple of Coors beers from her house, and we drank and goofed around for the better part of the day.

That summer, my family moved to Colorado and Laurie and I lost touch from that point on. Maybe that was a blessing.

Junior Prom photo 1974

Laurie Dann

By all accounts, Laurie had a pretty good senior year in high school. She dated the captain of the basketball team and her social life flourished. She went off to college and soon met the man of her dreams, Russell Dann, also from the Winnetka area. They married and appeared to have a storybook life together.

According to all the documentaries, tabloids, articles, books, and movies that have been written or produced about Laurie after May 20, 1988, she began struggling with mental illness in her 20s and it progressively got worse. Eventually, she sabotaged all her relationships, including her marriage, before spiraling down further into the depths of darkness.

My Struggle

While I lost Laurie Wasserman, my high school friend, on May 20, 1988, the rest of the world lost Laurie Dann, a psychotic school shooter and killer. I wanted to grieve the Laurie I knew, yet I also wanted to hate the Laurie she became. I was torn about how to feel. Without question, what Laurie Dann did to the community of Winnetka has left scars that will take a lifetime to heal. It was and still is horrific. But I didn't know that Laurie. The Laurie I knew was a much different person. She was my buddy and confidant. Talk about a conundrum!

What this story reveals to me is the seriousness of mental illness and the impact that it can have on so many people and so many communities. School shootings have increased, and mental health services are not being offered or utilized enough. We have a long way to go before the Laurie Danns of the world are getting the help they need.

Years later, when I had my talk radio show, I invited author Joyce Egginton on the show to talk about her book on Laurie Dann called, *Too Beautiful A Day to Die.* It was a fascinating interview with a surprise ending. To hear that show, go to my website, www.LeadingFromWithin.net.

13
Slip Sliding Away

*A mind stretched by a new experience can
never go back to its old dimensions.*

— Oliver Wendell Holmes

A colleague and I were waiting to be picked up in front of our San Francisco hotel when a man jogged by wearing nothing but running shoes. After a quick double take, a group of rambunctious women, wearing only strategically placed balloons, darted by. I turned to Krista, "Am I going crazy or did I just see a bunch of nakedness run by?"

Krista laughed, "Yes and yes! Actually, I'm still looking at the guy, so . . . "

Part of me was in a state of shock—while another part of me wanted to follow them to find out where they were going. *Is this simply life in San Francisco?* I wondered.

"I think it's a Halloween fun run," added Krista, apparently reading my mind.

"Wow, they sure know how to have fun here," I said, feeling disappointed that this was all happening as we're leaving for the airport.

"Have you ever done something like that?" she asked curiously.

"Wore balloons?"

"No silly, have you ever streaked before?"

Just then our cab pulled up.

"Saved by the bell!" I said as we got into the car.

She wasn't about to let this go. "You had to think about it. I think you have a story or two to tell me on the plane."

I smiled, thinking back to my freshman year in college. "Actually, I do have a streaking story. Just promise me it stays between us."

"No one except me and all of my Facebook friends will ever know!"

"In that case, I've never streaked."

"I'm just kidding," she pleaded. "Tell me."

My Streaking Story

Between my senior year in high school and my freshman year in college, streaking had become as popular on college campuses as toga parties and the movie *Animal House*. This wild-and-crazy phenomenon created very high expectations for many of us attending colleges at that time; expectations that rarely measured up to all the hype. My campus in particular was anything but *Animal House*. Our one lame fraternity didn't have a house and the social life in the dorms was virtually nonexistent. In fact, the only good parties were far enough off campus that you needed a car, which none of us as freshmen had. I guess you could say that our social life my first year was dead on arrival.

It was another boring Friday night. My buddies from my dorm stopped by to party and watch the paint dry.

"We need to do something," said Chas.

"We are," said Reed. "We're drinking beer and smoking weed with the boys!"

"Without chicks! Again!" winced Kent. "We're such losers!"

Tired of all the complaining, I jumped in. "I'm with Chas, let's make something happen."

"Should we have a party?" asked Reed.

"No, something different. We need to stir things up around here." And then an idea came to me. "We should streak!"

"Are you serious?" asked Kent.

"Why not," I added. "It happens on all the other campuses."

The idea began to sink in without any resistance from the group. The beer helped. The only downside was that none of us had ever streaked before and we weren't sure of all the particulars.

"Screw it," yelled Terry. "Let's just do it."

"No, no, no," I pleaded. "We need a plan."

"You guys, it's too cold out to streak," said Kent. "We need a different idea."

"Wait," said Terry. "Who said we have to streak outside. We could run through Ute Hall. It's all women."

"Why not," said Reed, with Chas nodding his approval. "We could undress in the basement of Ute Hall, hide our clothes, and then take the stairs and streak on the first floor and then the second, before going back down to the basement."

"We could be in and out in five minutes," I said.

"I'm in," said Kent, "but I'm going to wear my face mask. I don't want to be recognized."

Western State College resides in a very cold part of Colorado and most students had winter hats that pulled down into face masks to protect them from the bitter cold.

"Let's all wear masks," replied Chas. "My roommate and I have enough for everyone."

We all loved the mask idea, given that none of us wanted to stand out any more than we already would, if you catch my drift.

"We're really going to do this!" screamed Terry.

In the background was music from our one campus radio station, blaring from Kent's stereo. It gave me another idea. "Steve is the DJ tonight. What if we ask him to announce to all the women in Ute Hall to be out in the hallways at exactly 9:00 p.m. for a once-in-a-lifetime event?"

"Holy shit," said Reed. "You mean advertise that we're coming over? What about the element of surprise?"

"Who cares!" I reasoned. "What's the point of streaking if there is no one to see us?"

Everyone approved. The plan was coming together nicely. There would be five of us streaking and we'd undress in the basement before hitting the first floor and then the second. By our estimation, the whole round trip would take just a few minutes. It was perfect and certainly would stir things up around campus.

"I've got another idea," said Chas. "Why don't we take some water balloons with us and throw them at the women—you know, as a kind of distraction."

"I like it," I said. "It might take away some of the awkwardness for me."

"Me too," added Reed. "We can put them in a laundry bag and bring them over with us."

We were standing now, too excited to sit. We had about 45 minutes to get everything together and get over to Ute Hall.

"We've thought of everything, haven't we," cried Terry.

No response.

Most of it was a Good Idea

The partying continued as did our plan. DJ Steve made the announcement and we were on our way over to the basement of Ute Hall. As fun as this was going to be, I was surprisingly nervous when it came time to undress.

"We can't back down now," said Reed, as we put our face masks on and grabbed the water balloons.

The moment to back down had passed as Terry led the way up the stairs. There was a thick door that opened to the first floor and as he swung it open, we heard nothing but silence, followed by views of an empty corridor. It was completely deserted.

We all looked at each other in confusion.

"Steve announced we were coming, didn't he?" inquired Kent.

"Yes," I said. "I heard it myself."

"This is eerie," said Reed. "What if the whole building is deserted?"

We were walking down the corridor now, still thrown off by the emptiness.

"What do we do with our water balloons if no one is on the second floor either," asked Chas, rather dejectedly.

"We'll throw them all at Geese for having such a stupid idea," said Reed.

"It seemed like a good idea after the third beer," I mumbled apologetically.

Terry was still in front as we moved up the stairway to the second floor. By now our expectations had dwindled to the point that we'd all be happy with even a couple women in the hallway.

Terry grabbed the door. "You guys ready?"

We all nodded.

As he slowly opened the door, the cricket sounds that lined the first corridor magically erupted into a loud, rowdy stadium sound, like being on the football field when Alabama scores a touchdown, complete with cheering, chanting, and screaming. Cameras were flashing. The hallway was lined three people thick on each side with enthusiastic coeds ready for a show. It was so startling to us that we all panicked and started throwing our water balloons in every possible direction, including down the corridor. Large puddles of water covered the floor, creating the hazard of all hazards for novice streakers like us. The pandemonium heightened as one by one we all went down like a bunch of pins in a bowling alley, slip sliding down the hallway in various positions, while leaving nothing to the imagination.

Bruised and embarrassed, but with masks intact, we fled the second floor as fast as we could, screaming in glee as we ran down the stairs to the basement.

"We did it!" screamed Reed, as we were all giving each other high fives.

"I'd say we stirred things up on campus," I shouted.

The commotion coming from the second floor was getting louder. "Let's get out of here before anyone else sees us," advised Terry.

Later that Night

We got back to the room and immediately started rehashing our five minutes of fame. We were having so much fun bantering back and forth.

It was about 11:00 p.m. when we heard noise coming from the grassy quad area just outside our building. We rushed to the window. To our surprise, about 25 women from Ute Hall were lined up in front of our building, wearing bathrobes and chanting. Although we couldn't make out what they were saying, we'll never forget what we saw. One by one, each woman quickly opened and closed her bathrobe, revealing nothing underneath. After the last women flashed us, they all ran back into Ute Hall.

We were dumbfounded.

"What the hell just happened?" said Terry.

"Sweet Jesus," cried Reed. "I'm loving college!"

Part of me felt like a celebrity, even though no one knew who we were. And then it occurred to me, "Hey, how did they know to flash our dorm?" I asked curiously.

That part will forever remain a mystery. What mattered is that we achieved our objective. Western State College was never the same after that.

I looked over at Krista. "So that's my streaking story."

She shook her head. "You're so full of shit!"

We never spoke of it again—but I can't stop smiling every time I see her.

14
"Who's Paying You?"

*A mistake that makes you humble is better than
an achievement that makes you arrogant.*

— Unknown

I was asked to facilitate a two-hour focus group comprised of six people, to discuss a proposed recycling program in a nearby town. "Sure," I said, "how difficult could that be?" Granted I have never facilitated a focus group before, but six people—come on! Little did I know that in addition to the six people in the focus group there would be more than 200 angry community members also attending the meeting.

Note to self: Never assume anything.

The topic of recycling wasn't so much the controversial issue to the community members—it was the *mandatory* part that seemed to bring out every antigovernment entity around, including organizers from out of state.

As I walked into the city hall that night, the event coordinator ran up to me and said that the recycling issue had become somewhat heated since we had talked and that in addition to facilitating the small group of six, I also needed to address the growing crowd.

"Me?" I cried. "I thought you were going to do that?"

"I think you'd be better since you are a neutral party. Just explain the format and the ground rules," she insisted.

I looked at my watch. It was 6:25 p.m., and in five minutes this town-hall-meeting-gone-bad would begin! *This is going to be an agonizing two hours,* I thought to myself.

And it was.

Before I could even introduce myself to the rowdy crowd, a number of people began yelling and screaming at me. The loudest voice came from the back of the room, "Who's paying you?" By the second time he yelled it out, the room got uncomfortably quiet, as people waited to hear my response. I said, "I don't think that is relevant."

Oops, wrong answer. Then they got louder. Three or four people screamed together, "How much are you getting paid?"

Clearly, I was not viewed as a "neutral" facilitator. The angry crowd decided I had become "one of them,"—a representative of the city government. Fortunately for me, a member of city council inserted himself into the fury and defended the proposed recycling program. The good news was that the focus was finally off of me. The bad news was that the crowd was quickly getting out of hand.

I looked at my watch—it read 6:35 p.m. *OMG! It's only been five minutes. How am I going to survive this night?*

Eventually, the six focus group members and I were able to escape to another room, but not without members of the angry mob continuously disrupting our meeting by barging into the room and verbally attacking anything and everything we were doing.

When time was finally up for our focus group, I had the ugly task of going back to the larger room and reporting out on our findings to the agitated crowd. All I could think was, *be quick and get the hell out of here!*

As I entered the room for a second time, I was met with more shouting and constant disruption. I did my best, even though no one could hear what I was saying. There was no mic or sound system since this meeting was intended for a small group. I shouted as loud as I could and covered the summary points, while wondering if my car was safe out in the parking lot.

In the end, I was very thankful that people dispersed peacefully and that I was able to drive away with my car intact. I did learn some valuable lessons:

- The city council did a poor job in involving members of the community in this process, which caused a buildup of frustration.

- What triggered the community was not the recycling program itself, but the lack of transparency around it. Even the questions we were discussing in the focus group implied that the recycling program already had passed.

- I was embarrassed and ashamed for the lack of civility in the meeting and the comments directed at me. I understood the frustration but didn't appreciate how it was expressed.

- Oddly, as the night went on, I found myself agreeing more and more with the angry crowd. I objected with the city for not being open and honest with me about what to expect at the meeting.

- I walked into this gig blindly without doing my due diligence. Community issues can be very different than organizational issues. The stakes can be much higher and often impact a lot more people. This whole thing could have been handled much better on all of our parts.

- And lastly, I learned to always park close to the building for these events. You just never know when you might need to make a quick getaway!

15
The Standing Ovation!

*We cannot become what we need to
be by remaining what we are.*

— Max De Pree

I was out visiting my mother in St. Petersburg, Florida. It was late on a Friday afternoon and we were looking for something to do.

"How about going to the Don," mused mom. She was referring to the prestigious Don Cesar Hotel, often referred to as the *Pink Palace*.

"I guess," I said reluctantly. I thought we should try someplace new. The Don is one of our favorite places to hang out on St. Pete's beach, but I had spent a couple hours there earlier in the day watching the NCAA basketball tournament out at the pool bar.

"Or, we could go to that big old house that's now a restaurant," I offered. "What's that place called again?"

"You mean the Hurricane?"

"Yep, that's the one," I said. "Don't they have an outside bar on top of the roof?"

"Yes. We could go watch the sunset. Do you want do that?"

I couldn't agree fast enough. Besides, there was something else the Hurricane was known for, but I couldn't remember what. It had something to do with the rooftop bar and the sunset.

Spring Break in Florida

College students from around the country migrate to the beaches of Florida every spring to relax, bask in the sun, and party at the bars. And this day would be no different.

We got in the car and headed south. Sunset would be at about 7:30 p.m. and we were running late. It was 7:00 p.m. by the time we pulled up to the Hurricane, and, of course, there were no parking spaces to be found. *Why should this be easy*, I joked, as I dropped my mom off at the front of the restaurant. Surprisingly, she took everything in stride as she headed for the crowded elevator. "I'll see you up there."

As I searched for a parking spot, I felt a little guilty for dropping her off by herself. This was her first time out in St. Pete without my father, who had passed away just two months earlier. She was acting so strong—but I imagined she was concealing her grief and sadness. But that was mom. She rarely showed emotions and particularly didn't like to be vulnerable.

I definitely had my emotional moments over my dad's death; but, like my mom, I kept them to myself. Can you tell we're from the same family? In hindsight, I was trying to be strong for my family, and especially for my mom. But truthfully, I was uncomfortable to have an emotional moment with my mom, afraid I would trigger her sadness even more. So, to avoid that, I purposely tried to keep our conversations light and humorous.

By the time I parked the car and climbed up the stairs to the rooftop of the Hurricane, it was already 7:20 p.m. The rowdy crowd was partying like it was Mardi Gras in New Orleans, and the line to the bar had no end in sight.

So much for toasting the sunset, I thought, wondering how I'd find my mom in this sea of spring breakers.

Just then I heard a familiar voice off in the distance, "Greg, Greg, I'm over here." I looked in the direction of the voice, and there, to my surprise, was mom, sitting at a table with two drinks!

"How did you pull this off?" I said, as I sat down next to her.

Mom smiled and shook her head. "Gregory, you need to trust your mother."

I still don't know how she managed to secure a table and drinks among the crazy crowd, but figured my dad must have been looking after us. I raised my glass and looked at my mom. "Here's to Dad!"

By then, it was 7:30 p.m. and the sunset was well underway. Various shades of yellow, orange, blue, and gold all merged just above the heads of the hundreds of people who were all blocking our view.

"Do you mind if I stand on my chair so I can get a photo?" I asked.

"Go ahead. Just don't fall."

It was 7:38 p.m. The burnt orange sun was touching the edges of the water.

Sunset from the Hurricane

And then there was a hush.

It was like the crowd was in a trance; frozen in the moment. All eyes focused on the sun as it eased behind the gulf.

And then, right on cue, a loud roar erupted from our rooftop, as the sun ducked out of sight. I had goose bumps all over and glanced over at my mom. "Now I remember what the Hurricane is known for. They cheer the sunset!"

But my mom looked away to avoid eye contact. I looked closer and saw tears running down her cheeks. *Of course*, I remembered, *St. Pete sunsets were something my mom and dad had shared for more than 30 years.*

It was a quiet ride back to the condo. I had finally witnessed my mom being vulnerable and showing her emotions, and I searched for a way to redirect the conversation to something safer . . . again.

No wait, I thought, *I'm not going to pass this moment up. Too bad if I'm uncomfortable. It's time.*

"Were you thinking about Dad during the sunset?"

She nodded, "It's just been so hard."

And there it was: we finally began the conversation we both had been avoiding.

Afterthoughts

Prior to experiencing the sunset together at the Hurricane, I realized that rarely had I spent time (as an adult) alone with my mother. I was always with my mom and dad, or my mom and dad plus family members. This opportunity created an authentic moment for us to connect at a deeper level—something that had been missing for some time. I'm so grateful it happened. Sunsets at the Hurricane for me will never be the same.

16
The Sailing Trip from Hell

Life isn't about waiting for the storm to pass . . .
it's about learning to dance in the rain.

— Vivian Greene

The four-day trip around the Channel Islands, just off the coast of Southern California, started out like it was supposed to—calm seas, plenty of sunshine, and moderate wind speed of 18 to 20 knots. The channel was only about 35 miles across, which meant we would make safe harbor for the evening in five to six hours.

*Photo from fotolia by Adobe

The Backstory

I'm not a sailor. I love the idea of being a sailor, but the fantasy is much more appealing than the reality. The only other time I had sailed was a disaster. I had rented a sailboat at a nearby lake with some friends and the sailboat tipped over, propelling all of us into the cold water. As I tumbled over the side, my right shoulder popped out, leaving me in excruciating pain and with only one arm to dog paddle to the surface. It wasn't pretty, to say the least. We not only had to be rescued, but also I had to pop my own shoulder back in place. Ouch!

Perhaps you can understand why I was a bit hesitant when my buddies—Coy and Timmy—asked me to fly out to Santa Barbara with them for a three-day sailing excursion. But both were experienced sailors and assured me over and over again that they'd be doing the bulk of sailing.

The Sailing Trip

After motoring out of the Santa Barbara Sailing Center in a relatively new, 32-foot long Hunter sailboat, the swells were getting deeper as we moved out to sea. My crewmates seemed to welcome the challenge.

But soon, the wind picked up to 25 knots. I don't really know what that means, but it was starting to feel like an amusement ride gone bad—up and down and up and down! Fortunately, I had remembered to put on my sea sickness patch before we left. That was the good news. The bad news was that I had no idea how I would get to the little bathroom, let alone stand up in it, when that time came. Too much information?

The wind picked up to 30 knots as dark clouds filled the sky. With every swell and crash, all I could see was a wall of green seawater on all sides of us. I looked to my crewmates, hoping for reassurance, but I saw Timmy, hanging over one side of the boat, heaving whatever was left of his lunch. Coy frantically tried to sail the boat by himself, but he was in desperate need of assistance.

I watched the nightmare unfold. The wind howled as the angry ocean doused us over and over again with freezing seawater. My body was shaking from head to toe and I was unable to release my arms from the rail. The clouds were so low that it became difficult to see where the sky and sea separated. Up and down—left to right—up and down—left to right—with no end in sight. Without question, this was one of the most uncomfortable moments of my life. It was horrible!

The sea raged on for what seemed like hours. The winds were now over 40 knots and the swells over 18 feet tall. Timmy was so sick that he could no longer move from the fetal position. I wanted to help Coy, but the storm was so loud that I couldn't hear a word he said. And I wasn't about to let go of the rail. He was basically on his own.

Then, just at the apex of awfulness, we came upon the most amazing contradiction. A school of dolphins swam up alongside the boat. They jumped and played with glee.

The irony was overwhelming. *How could they be having such fun, when I'm literally experiencing the worst moment in my life!*

Photo from www.pinterest

But then a calmness came over me too. The dolphins were there to let me know that everything was going to be okay. It became clear that I needed to embrace the moment, lighten up, and enjoy the ride. It was so obvious that I laughed out loud.

The Aftermath

The five-hour trip took us nine hours, but the erratic seas finally calmed down and the sun reappeared in time for a beautiful sunset. That evening we laughed like little kids, reminiscing about the day's exhilarating voyage. To no surprise, we each had a different experience during those nine hours. For Coy, it was about sailing solo in treacherous seas. For Tim, it was about keeping his eye on the horizon and breathing. And for me, it was about loosening my grip and lightening up during difficult times. I have the dolphins to thank for that! Funny how what started out as the worst day ever turned into one of the best.

17
The Dating Game

Being perfect is being flawed, accepting it, and never letting it make you feel less than your best.

— Jessica Alba

* Written as a blog to promote one of our radio shows in 2014

Now, if you haven't noticed, today's show will be a departure from our traditional format. Instead of interviewing a guest about their latest book, Lisa and I will be asking dating questions to three bachelorettes calling in to the show in hopes of winning a date with me. I should mention that I'm using the word "hopes" loosely. For all I know, they may have been coerced to call in, although Lisa assures me that wasn't the case.

Lisa and me before our show

What I have found interesting about our Dating Game show being promoted on our radio website is that women I've either gone out with recently or that I'm trying to get a date with have mentioned it or questioned it. I think it is making them slightly apprehensive about going out with me. Imagine that! Who wouldn't want to go out with a guy who literally advertises on the radio that he wants a date? When did that stop being an attractive trait? I'm so confused.

Perhaps the Dating Game wasn't such a great idea after all.

It's weird being single again. Truthfully, I was never very good playing the dating game before I met my wife, so why should it be any different postwife. It seems like the older you get—okay, the older I get—the more particular I get as well. But that's not unusual, is it? And so what if I have a peculiarity or two? Who doesn't? I just need to find someone who thinks my quirky habits are cute, loveable, and not self-serving whatsoever! Hmm. Maybe I should just go out with myself.

I wonder if it's not too late to be a priest? Think about it—they get to give a speech every week, have meals cooked for them, and they're treated like celebrities when they wear their collar out in public. Just imagine how much I'd save on clothes! I wonder what the pay is?

But I'm not giving up just yet. They say the right person will show up when you're least expecting it. Yet, considering I haven't expected it, shouldn't she be here already? How long do I wait?

Do you ever watch other couples to try to determine if they have a good relationship or not? I do it all the time. Phone conversations are pretty revealing too, aren't they? It's not like I try to listen or eavesdrop to people's conversations, but it's not rocket science to sense if there is a positive or negative charge between two people's batteries. And we all know couples whose batteries are on low. After I got divorced, I anticipated having to explain to all inquiring minds why I got divorced and what went wrong.

Instead, most of my friends and family members told me they were not surprised. Was it that obvious?

I want to meet someone who makes me feel giddy again. I remember the first time I ever sat next to Carol Hook at a 6th grade basketball game. Every pore in my body radiated with infatuation. I could barely breathe. I had a crush on her for as long as I can recall but was too timid to ever talk to her. Here I was, sitting next to the woman of my dreams, and all I could say was, "So, who you pulling for?"

Really? First off, no one says *"Who you pulling for?"* Secondly, we went to the same school! But that's what I'm talking about. I was so dumbfounded that I could barely put a sentence together, let alone make any sense. I was giddy.

I want to feel that way again!

18
I Didn't Make the Short List

Friendship isn't about who you've known the longest. It's about who walked into your life, said, "I'm here for you," and proved it.

— Anonymous

When my friend Garry passed away, I was disappointed to be excluded from the small group of friends who got together to memorialize him. My disappointment wasn't just about not making his *short list*; I also regretted the way my relationship with him ended. Nothing happened; our relationship just slowly faded away, as many do. And yet, I probably think about him more now than I did when he was alive. Why didn't I make more of an effort to stay in touch, especially when I knew he was sick? Was that why didn't I make his short list?

I recently talked with a friend about the idea of the short list. He told me that, whether we know it or not, we all have a short list. As he put it, "These are the 'go-to' people in our lives." He referred to them as his *inner circle*.

Then he said, "If I were to ever get deathly sick, or to die, there are only a few people that I could really count on to be there."

"I would be there for you," I said.

"I know," he said. "That's why you're in the circle."

That was one of the most meaningful things someone has said to me in a while. *What an honor,* I thought.

In the movie, *Meet the Parents,* former CIA agent Jack Byrnes (played by Robert De Niro) has a *circle of trust.* For Jack, the circle included only trusted members of the Byrnes family. If you've seen the movie, you'll recall that Greg Focker (played by Ben Stiller) is continually moved in and out of the family's circle of trust due to his various antics.

Many years ago, I cocreated the Leading From Within workshop: a three-day experiential program in the mountains that focuses on authentic leadership. In that program, I took the circle of trust concept and expanded it into the *circle of friends,* using the popular Circle of Friends statue as our centerpiece.

Are you familiar with the story behind the statue?

The statue represents the bond that existed among the women from an ancient Indian tribe. As the story goes, each evening, after all the men and children had gone to bed, the women would gather together around the fire to love, honor, and appreciate each other. From their circle of friends ritual, the women drew the strength to transition from one day to the next.

Circle of Friends statue

In our workshop, we recreated the circle of friends whenever it was time to do personal and group sharing. The statue was symbolically placed in the center.

Here's the point I want to make with all of this.

Whether we call this selected group our *short list*, or our *inner circle*, or our *circle of trust*, or the *circle of friends*, we are referring to the people in our lives who:

- have our back;

- will unconditionally love and support us;

- will step in to help at a moment's notice; and

- are committed to being in relationship with us.

Now picture the circle of friends statue.

Imagine it's your circle and you are one of the seven people. Who are the other six? Who are the people in your life that you would place in your personal circle of friends and why? Do these people know how important they are? If not, why not?

I have a pretty good idea who is in my circle of friends. Most have been there for a while and know they are there. A few others have been very impactful in my life recently, so they don't yet know they are in my circle. I need to let them know.

I believe that we are all here on earth to discover and achieve our purpose, while helping others do the same. There is a reason we are in each other's lives. And we all need to do a better job of telling the people around us what they mean to us. No one should have to guess if we are on each other's short list.

19
A Costly Mistake

I told myself that I have to just keep on
breathing... for tomorrow the sun will rise...
and who knows what the tide will bring in.

— Tom Hanks in the movie, *Cast Away*

landed my dream job. It was early in my career,
but all I ever wanted was to work at a college or
university in Southern California. I can still feel the exhilaration
I felt when I was offered the director of student activities job at
Chapman College. When the call came, I was sitting in my cold
and windowless office at Washington University in St. Louis,
where I had just suffered through my second winter. I craved the
warm sun, palm trees, and the Pacific Ocean. That phone call was
the happiest moment of my life. I felt like I had won the lottery.

Chapman College (now Chapman University) is located in
Orange, California, just a hop and a skip away from the Newport
Beach area. The beautiful campus was dotted with palm trees and
collegiate white buildings. It smelled like fresh oranges. The students were fun, eager, and very active in extracurricular activities,

including the student government—for which I was the advisor. I reported to the dean of students and we had a tight connection.

About five months into the job, I was invited to accompany ten student government officers on a two-day retreat in Mission Bay, San Diego. Our agenda included planning sessions and trainings, mixed in with some fun and social time. Still on my California high, I pinched myself to make sure this wasn't a dream. *A student retreat in San Diego on the beach, are you kidding me! And this is just a typical day for these people!*

Mission Bay

Dressed in shorts, flip-flops and a T-shirt, I joined the students at our meeting space at the Beach Cottages, which included a picture window overlooking the boardwalk and the Pacific Ocean.

"I think I've died and gone to heaven," I shouted, as I positioned myself in a chair that faced the window. Because I was fairly new in my job, my role during the retreat was primarily to listen, learn, and offer advice. The students would run the retreat.

The first morning was great. Lots of creative ideas and participation from all the student leaders. I was impressed with each one of them and felt more and more connected to the group. We were having a good time. After lunch, we decided to have a touch football game on the beach for an afternoon activity. As the game became a little competitive, I overexerted myself and twisted my back. It was enough to cause spasms and great pain, thus ending the game. I assured everyone I would be fine: but I knew I was lying.

Back spasms were not new to me. Unfortunately, I had no medication, ice pack, heating pad, or walking cane—all accessories I'd used in the past. Lying down and staying in my room wasn't an option as I didn't want to miss a moment of this retreat. There were still two days to go, and I had to make it work.

It's awful to watch someone who is having back spasms. And it's even harder to experience that pain every 30-to-60 seconds. Finally, one of the students offered me one of their pain pills, which I gladly swallowed. It helped. I was able to make it through the afternoon session as the spasms subsided just enough so I could function. I was still worried.

Later, we met on the boardwalk in front of our hotel and walked along the beach to the restaurant we had selected for dinner. It was a quarter of a mile away and I was able to walk very gingerly, albeit with a tilt to the left to compensate for the irritation on my right side. A couple of the guys, Scott and Mike, walked with me while the rest of the group went ahead to secure a table.

Since our meetings were over until the following morning, I ordered a stiff drink to help loosen my back up. It really helped me relax enough to enjoy the company, a fine dinner, and the band playing in the next room. Things were feeling better.

It was about 10:00 p.m. when most of the group was ready to head back to the hotel. As I stood up, Scott pointed at me.

"Geese, we're going to hang out a little longer to see the next band. Stay with us."

I looked over at Mike who clearly was part of the "we." "Come on Geese-man, I'm staying," he said, nodding his head.

I smiled, happy to be included. "Why not, what harm could there be."

The Bonfire

Scott was the editor of the college student newspaper. He was actually my age, but choose to go into the military for a few years before college. We had a lot in common and I enjoyed his company. Although a student, he seemed more like a friend to me. Mike, on the other hand, was a goofy 21-year-old senior who was one of the funniest people I've ever met. He frequently would be entertaining students around campus with his stand-up jokes and humorous monologues. He was a good guy who loved hanging around me for some reason.

It was 11:45 p.m. and the restaurant was closing. The three of us were finishing up with a really nice and meaningful conversation when we decided to head back by way of the beach. My back was pretty stiff by now, but at least the spasms were holding off.

As we walked along the ocean with the most amazing stars beaming down at us, we came across a small bonfire where three guys were relaxing and drinking beer. Mike immediately walked over to say hello and quickly called us over for introductions. The three guys were just back from deployment from the Gulf War. They were Air Force pilots from Operation Desert Shield, the largest military alliance since World War II. We were blown away! These were military heroes.

After introductions, the airmen invited us to join them for a beer. Although we were pretty spent from the long day and evening, we couldn't find a compelling reason to turn in just yet and happily joined them around the fire. As we talked, each of the airmen shared their stories and experiences from the war. It was intense and amazing at the same time, giving me goosebumps being in their presence. I recall feeling like a little kid meeting a famous sports hero. I couldn't get enough.

After about 20 minutes, one of the airmen pulled out a joint and lit it. I looked over at Mike just as the joint was passed to him. He ignored my stare and took a hit before passing it on to Scott. Scott followed suit, took a hit and passed it on to me. I smiled, reflecting on how this may very well be one of the coolest moments in my life, and took a hit and passed it on. It just felt right to me. Unfortunately, that mind-blowing moment would prove to be the beginning of the end of my career at Chapman College.

Back on Campus

A number of weeks had passed since the student government retreat when the dean of students called me into her office.

"I don't know how to say this," she lamented, "so I'm just going to say it. I'm going to have to ask you to resign at the end of the school year."

My mouth dropped. "What? Why?"

I could see how painful the conversation was for her. She continued. "I could defend you for botching a program or for missing an important meeting—or anything like that—but I cannot defend you for smoking marijuana with students at a student event."

I had never been fired from anything before and was having trouble catching my breath. So many thoughts were flooding through me. *How did she find out? Do I defend myself? Should I call a lawyer?* And worst of all, *What do I tell my parents?*

"But Susan," I pleaded, "I was in severe back pain. The student event had ended hours ago, and I simply took one hit off a joint—which came from the Air Force pilots we were sitting with on the beach in the middle of the night."

"It doesn't matter, Greg. You were smoking pot with students and word has gotten to Hans." She paused. "He wants you out."

Hans was the vice president for student affairs and Susan's boss. He was a very conservative and rigid guy with very low tolerance for any wrongdoing, whether from students, staff, or faculty.

After she mentioned Hans, I knew that there was nothing I could say that would change the outcome of this conversation. I had messed up big time and now my California dream was crashing in on me. I had no one to blame but myself.

The Aftermath

Mike and Scott felt terrible. Mike never intended to get me in trouble when he shared our experience with the airmen to hundreds of his closest friends. Scott was so upset that he met with Susan and took full responsibility for everything that happened, but to no avail. Susan's hands were tied. For me, it was yet another lesson learned the hard way. I should have known better than to smoke an illegal substance while representing the college, but I was so caught up in the moment that I made a bad decision. That's on me.

I was able to finish out the academic year and attend graduation and various end-of-the-year festivities. I had time to say my goodbyes and my relationship with Susan stayed strong. By mid-May, I had officially resigned from the college and managed to find a job on the beach managing an ice cream franchise in Irvine, California. Although the pay was the same, wearing a beanie every day and serving ice cream to kids was a constant struggle for my ego. The beanie put me over the edge.

After about three months—and a hernia operation from carrying massive containers of ice cream all summer—I came across a job opening for the same position that I had at Chapman College but at the University of Redlands, only about 45 minutes away. Could this be a possible second chance?

I applied.

Two weeks later I received a call from the dean of students at the University of Redlands asking me to come in for an interview. I was ecstatic. My only challenge was figuring out how I would explain my departure from Chapman College. But, it was an opportunity to correct a past wrongdoing. I was all in.

The Do-Over

The University of Redlands was a much larger university than Chapman and even more beautiful. It was surrounded by mountains and the community of Redlands had a very intimate feel. It was so alluring that I became increasingly nervous as I walked around campus to prepare myself for the interview. Usually when I want something this bad, something goes wrong. Would this be one of those times?

The dean was waiting at the door for me along with two members of her staff. It was summer and most of the students and faculty were away for break, leading to a very relaxed and informal atmosphere. We headed to the conference room.

The interview itself went as well as I hoped. My one year at Chapman gave me enough experience that I could respond to questions with thoughtful insights and examples that only an experienced student activities director could deliver. We laughed, we shared stories and we connected. It was perfect—except for the elephant in the room that was looming over the interview.

Do I bring it up, I wondered, *or not say a thing unless asked?* I didn't know what to do, so I did nothing.

The interview came to an end. As I was shaking hands and thanking everyone for the interview, the dean asked me to step in her office for a moment.

Oh crap, I thought, *here's where the tire meets the road.* I started sweating as I sat in a chair directly facing the dean.

"I wanted to share something with you," she said.

I braced myself.

She pulled out a letter. "This is from Susan, your former boss. I wanted to read to you what she had to say."

I started panicking. I didn't realize the two had conferred already. *This is not going to be good!*

She began.

> *"I wanted to let you know that I fully recommend Greg Giesen for the director of student life position. I've never met anyone that cares so much for the student and who is willing to do whatever is necessary to provide exceptional services and programs for them.*

Granted, he has made some mistakes, as any new professional will do from time to time, but his integrity and desire to do the right thing always wins out.

In short, you cannot go wrong by hiring this young man.

Please call with any questions. Sincerely, Susan."

I almost cried in that moment. It blew me away for Susan to endorse me so heartily. I've never felt so blessed.

The dean smiled, knowing I'd be surprised and relieved. Clearly, she had thought all of this out in advance. Then she said to me, "We'd love to have you join our team!"

I couldn't say "yes" fast enough. It was the second chance I had hoped for!

20
Who Are You?

When you empty yourself of the illusions
of who and what you think you are, there
is less to lose than you had feared.

— Carol Osborn

I t seemed like a simple enough exercise, so I stood
up and went to the front of the room.

"Who are you?" shouted the group, in a seemingly respectful
manner.

"I am a leadership development coach," I proudly replied.

"No," responded a gentleman from the front row. "We didn't
ask what you do, we asked, who are you?"

"I'm Greg," I said, a bit confused now.

"No, that's your name. Who are you?" said the woman with
bright red hair from the back.

"Um, I'm a 56-year-old man?" My response was more of a question, as I looked for some kind of indication of what they were after.

Another woman from the back jumped in. "We didn't ask
about demographics, we asked, who are you?"

The group seemed to be getting agitated with me now.

"Ah, let's see, I'm someone who hates this exercise right now," I joked, totally lost.

Dead silence.

An older man stood up and approached me in front of the group. He smiled and softly said, "Yes, I can see you are uncomfortable, but who are you?"

"I'm frustrated, that's who I am. Who are you?" I shot back.

"No, this is about you," said a bald man in the second row. "Who are you?"

I could see that they weren't going to let up. I needed a different response.

"I'm vulnerable, I'm confused. I need some guidance here," I pleaded.

"So, then who are you?" said a young man from the front row.

Okay, I thought to myself, *I can figure this out.* "Who do you want me to be?"

"Who are you?" shouted the group, clearly getting impatient.

I shook my head in desperation. "I am a loving, honest, and caring person—that's who I am!"

Suddenly, all 40 participants were cheering and clapping. "Yes! Now you got it!" I looked up in surprise, like I had just discovered I held the winning lotto ticket.

I smiled and headed back to my seat, high fiving everyone on my way. I glanced at the man sitting next to me and said, "Wow, that was a lot harder than I imagined."

He put his arm around me, "Yes, but you did it! Nice job."

So, Who Are You?

We think we know ourselves, but do we really? Whenever I've done that exercise with a group, the responses, much like in my story above, always start out with titles, roles, responsibilities, and any other external traits that people can come up with to define who they are. Why is that? In my opinion, it's because many of us haven't taken the time, nor allowed the time, to do more in-depth analysis of who we are, let alone being able to put that definition into words.

Does it matter?

Yes! It really matters because when we allow our titles, roles, and responsibilities to define who we are, we narrow our essence down to labels. We all are much more than our name, or profession, or marital status. Those descriptors may paint us on the outside, but they certainly don't define who we are on the inside.

So, who am I, you ask?

I am a passionate and caring man committed to living, loving, laughing, and learning—and helping others do the same!

Yep, that's who I am.

And who are you?

21

The Marathon That Would Never End

All great players know there are days when,
no matter what they do, the game wins.

— Richard Coop

When it comes to asking for help—I simply won't do it. Actually, that's not completely true. I will ask for help, but only as a last resort, after I've exhausted every other option.

Carol and I were running buddies. Back in the 90s, we were in the same running club and often ran together during the weekly interval training. Over time, we became friends and would even do our long runs together on the weekends. I was in training for my first marathon in Boulder, Colorado, and was grateful to have Carol to train with. She had run numerous marathons and triathlons and was a great resource on everything from my diet to the number of miles I needed to train each week.

But what I failed to plan for, or train for, or ask about, was the actual terrain of the Boulder marathon. Although I was in the best shape of my life, it never occurred to me to train at higher elevations or the steep grades that I would face in Boulder.

The Boulder Marathon

I'll never forget that day. Though the sun was shining, the winds were against us at 30 to 50 mph. There I was, trying to run up a mountain (that I never trained for) with a wind (that I never anticipated) literally pushing me back down. It was like running in slow motion while exerting twice the amount of energy. Not even a mile into the race, I knew I was in trouble as more and more runners passed me with what looked like minimal effort. *How are they doing that,* I thought, as my frustration turned inward. *Why didn't I prepare for this! Why didn't Carol say something!* Between fighting the winds, the ascending roads, and my negative thoughts, I was falling apart.

And then it got worse.

Completely exhausted, I somehow managed to make it to the 13-mile mark (the halfway point), but my body was struggling. The lactic acid build-up in my quads made every stride so painful that walking was the only way I could move forward. The marathon was beating me into the ground, and I didn't know what to do. What's worse, I came alone to the marathon. There was no Carol, no support team, or any marathoners to run with for encouragement. They had all passed me up a long time ago.

And on it went. I trudged in pounding pain. I limped, I cursed—but I kept moving. At the rate I was going, I knew I wasn't going to finish the race, but it was more painful to stop than to keep walking. So I kept moving—albeit at a snail's pace. By mile 20, I couldn't go any further and collapsed right there on the road. I had nothing left in the tank and the pounding in my legs was so intense that all I could do was rock myself back and forth and wait for help.

About 15 minutes later, a flatbed truck pulled up. It was the race organizers and they had to scrape me up and help me into the back of their truck. To my surprise, I found three other runners there in the same condition as I was. *Well at least I beat those guys,* I mused to myself. We then drove the rest of the course to the finish line, where a crowd had gathered to cheer for the runners—and for us. We each received a "participation" medallion as we got out of the truck. Now I know how those kids feel who get trophies just for showing up at the school tournament. A very hollow feeling to say the least.

Days Later

I couldn't walk. Okay, maybe that's a bit of an exaggeration; I could walk but not without a lot of pain. But the pain paled in comparison to my disappointment over not finishing the marathon. It felt like I had just tossed three months of training down the drain and all I had to show for it was a lame participation medallion.

Then, four days after my aborted attempt, an outlandish idea came to me while I was getting a leg massage. I grabbed my cell and called Carol.

"You're going to do what?" she yelled. "You're absolutely crazy!"

Carol wasn't buying my logic. I tried again. "It is no different than doing a long run just before a marathon," I pleaded.

"You can barely walk. That's not the same!"

My pain was bearable, and I knew I'd be fine by the weekend, when the Pueblo marathon was scheduled to take place. I was convinced that I could do another marathon, as long as it was on a flat course. Plus, I just couldn't let three months of training go down the drain without a completed marathon. I just couldn't.

"But I'm going to need your help," I added.

"You definitely need help," she joked.

I smiled. "Funny—but I'm serious. I need you to come with me to Pueblo."

"I'm not running a marathon," Carol shot back.

"I know, Carol. What I need is for you to run the last six miles with me. Will you do that?"

I could tell by her tone of voice that she was going to say yes.

"I actually think that is a very good idea, especially considering your condition," she added. "Okay, I'll go with you."

I knew that enrolling Carol as my support team was the right thing to do. I should have done it the week before. *Why do I always learn things the hard way?* I thought to myself as I ended our call.

Little did I know what lie ahead . . .

Marathon 2

The sun was just coming up from the east. It was 6:00 a.m. and a cool 45 degrees outside. Carol wanted to run the first two miles with me before taking off for a leisurely breakfast. She was enjoying the whole experience.

"I'll meet you at the 20-mile mark in about three hours, okay?" she said as she trailed off from the course.

I nodded, quietly wondering if I could run the next 18 miles in three hours. Clearly my confidence wasn't where it needed to be.

This was a much smaller field of runners from the 400+ in Boulder the week before. In one sense, it was nice to have so much room between runners. In another sense, I could literally run for a mile or two and not see a single person. It was kind of eerie. Negative thoughts began passing through my head. *What if I get into trouble? Will anyone be able to find me?* And then a more disturbing thought, *I have no way to contact Carol should something happen before mile 20! I didn't bring my phone.*

Marathons have a way of playing mind games with you, especially if you are in any kind of pain. And, as self-fulfilling prophecies go, by the time I hit the 13-mile mark, the lactic acid build-up came back with a vengeance. The pain was excruciating. Panic came over me as the course moved through a dense forest. *No! This can't be happening!*

By mile 14 it was *déjà vu* all over again. I couldn't run any longer and was forced to walk. I wondered what was worse—the intense pain in my legs or the intense disappointment I was feeling. It was like I was watching the same bad movie two weeks in a row, unable to change the channel. I couldn't even muster the energy to look up and acknowledge the few stragglers as they passed me by. I was in serious jeopardy of not finishing the marathon—again!

I looked at my watch. The three-hour timeframe to meet Carol had already passed. She was waiting for me at mile 20, but I had no way to tell her that I was only at mile 17 and walking. The temperature was now over 90 degrees as the course moved to the open desert. There was no shade in sight, nor were there runners, or race officials, or even a truck to scrape me up. At this point, whatever pride I had left was long gone. Now it was about survival—and that meant I had to get to mile 20. There was no other way to end the nightmare.

Slowly, methodically, I put one leg in front of the other and kept moving. Walking had never been so difficult. As mile 19 came and went, I could feel my hopes rise. *Surely, I can make it one more mile.*

And then, off in the far distance, I could see the 20-mile marker, the same mark that did me in the previous week. But at least Carol would be there to help me. I was an hour-and-a-half late at this point and most likely dead last in the race.

As I approached with agony written all over my face, I noticed an ambulance was parked on the left side of road, obviously waiting for the last runners to either pass by or hop in the back. And there on the right side, with a big smile on her face, was Carol, looking at me as if I had just come back from the dead. What a welcome sight!

She gave me a big hug and helped me over to a shaded area where we sat down. My emotions were overflowing as I lamented about my aches and pains and the physical toll the last seven miles had taken on me. My legs were aching so much that I had to rock back and forth in an attempt to distract myself from the pain.

"What do you want to do?" she asked, very concerned.

"I can't go on. This whole thing was a bad idea," I cried out.

Carol squeezed my arm. "We don't have to do anything right now, let's just sit here for a while."

"I blew it," I said, shaking my head. "You told me I was crazy and I ignored you. I'm sorry."

Another 20 minutes passed. Just then the ambulance pulled out and took off down the road. Carol and I looked at each other and immediately started laughing.

"Now I'm really screwed," I joked.

Carol got up and looked over at me. "Hey, why don't we just walk a little together," as she pointed toward mile 21. "We can quit at any time—but my car is in that direction anyway."

Feeling a little better, I agreed. "As long as we have to go that way anyway, why not."

The 20th mile of the Pueblo marathon will always go down as a turning point for me. Had Carol not been there, I would have given up on my dream and taken a ride in the back of the ambulance. But Carol *was* there, and here we were walking toward mile 21, chatting away as good friends do, one step after the other.

When we came up to the 21-mile mark, my legs were pounding so bad that I was forced to sit down again. "Where did you park the car?" I asked, while rocking back and forth.

She looked at me apologetically, "Near the finish line. But don't worry, we can catch a ride over there."

We sat for 20 more minutes.

"Do you want to try walking again?" she asked.

By now the pulsating feeling had subsided. "Sure. We have to go that way anyway," I said again, trying to be funny while seriously wondering if we'd ever reach the 22-mile mark on foot.

We slogged on for what seemed like the longest time.

"At this rate, I don't think we're going to ever see mile 22," I complained, wondering how we were going to "catch a ride" as Carol suggested.

"Over there!" points Carol.

I look up and couldn't believe my eyes. It was the mile 23 marker!

"No way!" I exclaim. "Where did mile 22 go?"

Carol looked at me with a smile, "We passed it already and you didn't notice. Greg, we can do this!"

"Do what?"

"We can finish this marathon," she said.

I resisted. "I can't make three more miles. Carol, let's just get out of here. I'm done with this."

"That's fine," she said. "I just thought that since we are so close that maybe . . . "

"Maybe what?"

"Greg, since mile 20 we've already walked over three miles. Remember, we're doing this together. Just three more miles and we'll be at the finish line."

I was almost convinced. "Do you think we can? I mean, do you think I can?"

"We're doing it now," she says.

I perked up. A long, lost skip appeared in my step. I started to imagine the finish line instead of the car as my final destination. I actually started to jog!

The adrenalin that pulled me through all those months of marathon training took over. We made it through mile 24 and then mile 25. Five hours had passed since the start of the race and we were merging onto Main Street in downtown Pueblo in a full-out run for the finish line. City workers cheered us on (while picking up the cones behind us). Cars honked. Runners who finished hours earlier passed us in the other direction, giving us high fives.

"We are going to do this," I scream.

"I told you," shouted Carol as she veered off the course and watched me cross the finish line.

I did it! We did it! And once I crossed the line, I was presented with the same exact participation medallion that I got the week before!

I embraced Carol, with tears rolling down my face. For Carol, it was just an ordinary Saturday in the park, helping out a friend. For me, it was so much more. It was about friendship; it was about asking for help; it was about perseverance; it was about overcoming adversity; and it was about finishing my first and last marathon ever!

Thank you, Carol! You have no idea how eternally grateful I will always be.

22
My Park Bench

*Pay attention to the questions you need to
ask, not the answers you want to hear.*

— Leonard Hirsch

I have my very own park bench. Actually, it's not just a bench—it's a memorial bench. That's right, I have a memorial bench and I'm not dead (yet).

Allow me to explain.

For all of my adult life, I have been a regular visitor to Wash Park, without question the best park in Denver. It's nestled in a quaint and upscale neighborhood south of downtown and draws an attractive array of visitors: be it walkers, runners, bikers, volleyball players, and simply park lovers, like me. On the northeast corner of the park, there is a small lake (more like a pond) that offers the most amazing view of the boathouse, framed by the majestic Colorado mountains off in the distance. This has been my favorite spot at the park. I've even joked with my friends that when I die, I'd like my memorial bench to be right there.

The perfect spot for a bench

A number of years ago, a good friend of mine passed away from cancer. He and his wife loved Wash Park and also spent a lot of time there. Upon his death, his wife decided to honor him by purchasing a memorial bench on the south side of the park. His bench sits in front of another small lake, also facing the mountains, making for an amazing picturesque view.

Months after my friend's death, I ran into his wife at Wash Park, and we walked over to her husband's memorial bench to check it out. As we talked, I inquired about the steps involved in purchasing a memorial bench. She gave me the name of the person in charge at the Parks Department and asked why I was so interested.

"I'm just curious," I said. "I also wanted to know if they let you reserve benches."

"You want to reserve a bench? For who?"

"Me." I replied.

"Okay, that's weird," she said.

"I know it's weird, but people preselect their gravesites. How is that any different?"

She looked at me like I was crazy. "Well, good luck with that."

I smiled. "I'm just going to call and see what they say. What have I got to lose?"

Careful What You Ask For

"Yes, hi. My name is Greg Giesen and I'd like to inquire about a memorial park bench at Wash Park."

"Okay, Mr. Giesen, I can help you with that," said the woman from the Park Service.

Relieved to be talking to the right person, I continued. "Can I pick the bench or is it assigned?"

"If a bench is still unmarked, you can select it," she replied.

"Great. Do you happen to know if the bench on the southeast corner of the park in front of Smith Lake is still available?"

She paused as she checked her records. "Let's see, there is a double bench at that spot . . . and yes, it is available."

"I'll take it," I said, surprising even myself.

"I can do that for you," she says again, this time a little more formally. "And who is it for?"

Realizing that I hadn't thought this all out, I stumbled. "Ah . . . it's for . . . it's for . . . my dad," I replied, too embarrassed to admit it was for me.

She continued. "Okay. And what's your dad's name?"

Here we go! I thought. *This is where I get caught.* "Um . . . his name is the same as mine."

"So, his name is Greg Giesen Sr., correct?"

"Well, yes, but he preferred Greg Giesen instead of Greg Giesen Sr. He was funny that way."

She was on to me. "But that's your name?"

"I know, I know," I reasoned. "But can't we just leave it as Greg Giesen?"

"Mr. Giesen, you cannot purchase a memorial bench for yourself; so if it's for your dad by the same name, then it has to be Greg Giesen Sr."

"Okay, I guess we can leave it that way," I said reluctantly.

"Great. Email me what you would like on the memorial plaque and we'll get started on it."

As I hung up, the excitement for my bench was overshadowed with a slew of negative self-talk. *I thought I was just getting information. What ever happened to reserving the bench? Why did I give her my name? Shouldn't I have planned this out before calling? How am I going to explain Greg Giesen Sr.?*

And yet, as the days passed, I became more and more at peace with the whole thing. After all, I succeeded in obtaining my bench at my favorite spot in the park, which was huge. And for the Greg Giesen Sr. faux pas, that story would simply add to the folklore of my bench.

With the bench locked in, the inscription was the next critical part to figure out. All of the benches at Wash Park have either quotes or words of remembrance inscribed on their memorial plaques. In each case, the message was about the person being memorialized.

I wanted something completely different. I wanted people to reflect upon *their lives,* not mine, while sitting at the bench. To do this, I decided to ask a two-part question on the inscription:

The inscription at my bench

My hope was that the questions will invite people to reflect, discuss, debate, or even challenge themselves around the topic of passion and how it shows up in their lives. After all, I consider myself to be a very passionate person, and I use that passion to guide everything I do.

The plaque in front of my bench was completed and cemented in place in 2003. A few years later, I received an interesting call from Candice, a woman who is a resident in the Wash Park area. She was trying to track down Greg Giesen Sr., or a direct descendent. She wanted to share her story about the park bench. Here is her story:

I was a very successful businesswoman who owned seven companies. I lived in the Wash Park neighborhood with my two dogs, who I regularly walked in the park. The year was 2016 and I became deathly ill, barely able to work, let alone take care of myself. I became very concerned about my health, my career, and my life. Then one day, as I mustered enough energy to take my dogs to the park, I felt faint and had to sit down on the closest park bench. Turns out it was Greg Giesen Sr.'s bench. Feeling exhausted, depressed, and very emotional, I began to cry and put my head into my hands. When I opened my eyes, I noticed the questions on the plaque next to my feet. I read and reread the questions, realizing I had lost my passion in my life and that was the reason I was feeling so disconnected from everything. I had lost touch with the things that mattered to me. That insight ended up being a life-changing moment for me and helped me turn my health and my life around.

When Candice and I met up, she was pretty surprised to learn that I was the same Greg Giesen whose name was inscribed on the plaque. We had a good laugh about the coincidence of meeting, via my bench, followed by a meaningful conversation about purpose and passion.

Candice's story confirmed for me the decision to go with questions on my memorial plaque. It also revealed to me that my bench is serving a purpose. People get to work on themselves while sitting on my bench. It's the kind of legacy I'm proud to leave behind . . . and yet still experience for myself. How cool is that!

23

Getting "Schooled" By My Students

Example is not the main thing in influencing others, it's the only thing.

— Albert Schweitzer

I was cofacilitating a week-long outdoor leadership program in the mountains of Colorado. The program was designed to enhance the abilities of up-and-coming leaders who already were in positions of responsibility within their respective organizations. The group consisted of 20 participants from around the country, ranging from 22 to 35 years old.

On the first day of this program, we introduced a competition that would last throughout the week. At week's end, we would present an award to the most outstanding participant who exemplified the leadership proficiencies and traits that we'd be teaching. The winner would be decided by the participants and would be presented with an award at the closing activity.

The reason we announced the award on the first day was twofold. First, we wanted to send the message that every day counts when it comes to leadership: including relationships, effort, communication, and self-awareness. We hoped that a little competition would serve as an incentive to bring out the best in everyone. Second, and rather selfishly, we needed volunteers during the week to lead various activities and group discussions. We figured the award might also inspire participants to step up and volunteer. It did.

As expected, the energy within the group was consistently high throughout the week. We had so many participants initiating and volunteering that we had to find special jobs for everyone to do. It was a nice problem to have. These leaders were trying to stand out from the pack.

One participant surprised me, though. Stuart was the exception to the rule. Despite being in a leadership program, never once did he volunteer for anything.

Normally, such a dynamic would concern me. How could someone like Stuart learn to lead by not leading? How would he get anything from the program? And was it fair to the rest of the group for Stuart to sit back while they did all the leading?

To be fair, Stuart wasn't exactly a slacker. He was always very engaged with the group and the task at hand. If ever someone needed help, it was Stuart who volunteered. He also made an effort to sit with different members from the group during meals throughout the week. Maybe a small thing, but it did catch my eye.

Fast forward to the last day of the program—a day reserved for reflection, celebration, and selecting that one leader for recognition. Participants would not only select the winner, but they also had to come up with the selection process. We had so many quality leaders who really stepped up all week, I expected it to be a tough decision.

Based on past experiences with this program and this particular activity, I knew it could take the group a while to complete this assignment. Normally, I'd have enough time to pull out my novel and find a comfortable spot under a tree to relax and read—but something caught my attention. Off in the distance I could see a couple members of the group walking my way. *Hmm,* I said to myself, *I thought my instructions were as clear as day. What do they need me to explain again?*

"How can I help?" I said as they approached.

"No help needed," said Paul. "We're done."

"Now that's funny," I replied, knowing that there's no way a group of twenty could make such a quick decision. "Seriously, what do you need?"

Marlene, the other designated person, said, "Greg, we did what you asked. We selected one person, per your instructions, who best demonstrated the leadership traits and characteristics that we've been studying all week."

"But you barely had time to gather. How could you make a decision so quickly?" I inquired.

"Because it was an easy decision," replied Paul.

Still not trusting what I was hearing, I asked, "Okay, humor me. Who did you pick?"

In unison, they said, "Stuart."

"Wait, who?"

"Stuart," said Marlene.

I shook my head in confusion. *They didn't say what I just heard them say, did they?* I was feeling a little irritated now. "Let's see if I got this right. You selected the one person who never once led during the week as the person who best exemplified the traits and characteristics of a leader? Is that what I'm hearing?"

They both nodded.

"Greg," cried out Paul, "we chose Stuart because he led from the inside out. He led through his individual connections. He led through his unending support of all our efforts. He led by bringing everyone together for a common cause. And he did this simply by being himself. He is as authentic as they come."

"Yeah but he never stepped up and led the group," I reminded them again.

"Not all leaders lead from the front of the line," said Marlene.

"I know that," I said, surprised to hear her say something that I would typically say.

They explained that through his authenticity, Stuart became the heartbeat that held the group together—and always without fanfare or recognition. He wasn't trying to lead; he was just being himself.

I was very impressed with their rationale. They were telling me something I knew but somehow had forgotten.

As I drove home that day, I had to admit that I'd just been schooled by my students. They reminded me that we all can be leaders, regardless of whether we are at the front or the back of the line. Stuart knew who he was and didn't try to be anything or anyone different. He provided connection, support, and integrity—and he clearly impressed the whole group in the process.

24
Departures

> Life should not be a journey to the grave with the
> intention of arriving safely in an attractive and
> well-preserved body, but rather to skid in
> sideways—a scotch in one hand—chocolate in
> the other—body thoroughly used up, totally
> worn out and screaming, "Wow, what a ride!"
>
> — Hunter S. Thompson

lost my father in 2012 and my mother in 2014. In both cases, I was able to be with them in their final moments and to tell them I loved them before they passed. What follows are my thoughts and feelings around the time of their deaths.

My Dad

When it's my time to go, I want to emulate my dad during his final days. It was the night we contracted with hospice and learned my dad had just a few days to live. The mood was solemn, bleak, and very emotional for our family—except for my dad, that is. He was actually working the room, as if on stage or sparring with friends. It was such a contradiction that I pulled out my pen to record what was happening.

The hospital nurse said to my father, "Sign here so we can treat you."

"I want to see what the treats are first," retorted my dad with a smile.

Moments later the hospice nurse approached my dad and said, "John, we need to know who you'd like to be the back-up decision maker to your wife, in case she is not available."

Without even blinking, my dad, a far-right Republican, looked around the room at all of us before replying, "I want President Obama."

Then the hospital administrator came into the room to finish his paperwork and asked my dad, "Mr. Giesen, we need to know about the whereabouts of your Living Will."

On a roll now, my dad countered, "It's in the shoe box under my bed."

I couldn't believe any of this. The tears I anticipated were not coming from sorrow but from laughing at my dad's constant one-liners. I felt like I should have jumped in and said, "He's here all week! Be sure to tip your waiters and waitresses."

I used to think that dad's one-liners were kind of corny, until I realized the impact they had on others. They lightened the mood, made people laugh, brought out people's smiles, and helped everyone loosen up and take themselves a little less seriously.

Not a bad legacy if you ask me.

As the days passed, my dad's health continued to decline at a rapid pace. To no surprise, my last conversation with him ended with him saying to me, "Gregory, never lose your sense of humor."

A couple days later, my father slipped into a comatose state. Although he seemed to be at peace, his breathing was very inconsistent.

My dad working the room at his 80th birthday party

We all looked at the hospice nurse, "Can't you do anything for him?"

She reassured us, "That's very normal and part of the process. His body is slowly shutting down."

I was having a difficult time seeing my father in this state. I kept waiting for him to wake up and deliver the next one-liner, but it never came. The whole family was around him now, some crying, some in shock.

The hospice nurse could tell his time was near and suggested we each say our final goodbye and give him permission to go. My mother, married to my father for over 60 years, held my father's face, kissed him and said, "I love you John Giesen. It's okay to go now."

Just then, a tear formed from one of my father's closed eyes and rolled down his cheek. My mother broke down, as did the rest of us. It was one of the most touching moments I've ever seen and one I'll never forget.

We all took turns saying our final goodbyes and giving him permission to go.

My father's last breath was at 8:48 a.m. on Saturday, January 14, 2012. He left this earth with the same smile on his face that I bet he came in with, more than 83 years ago. And although there was no more laughter or one-liners coming out of room 4125, there was a tremendous amount of love in the room to fill the void.

My father was a great man and will be missed.

My Mom *(just before her passing, two years later)*

Two years prior, I'd had the privilege of witnessing my father's death and dying process. Although a bittersweet experience, it meant a lot to me to be with him during his final hours, along with the rest of my family.

As I write about my mother's final chapter of life, a strong sense of déjà vu overwhelms me. The similarities are uncanny.

There is so much I want to say—and yet the weight of my heavy heart makes it difficult to press on the keys of my laptop, let alone stay focused. The last two weeks have been an emotional rollercoaster, filled with love, sadness, appreciation, and grief.

It's been too much at times.

When my father died, much of my sorrow was pushed to the side so I could attend to my mother and help fill the gap left by his sudden death. That focus prevented me from having complete closure from his passing; which probably explains why I'm feeling like I'm losing them both right now. They were always such a sweet pair together.

The last two years had been particularly difficult for my mom. She not only lost her partner and best friend, but she also was thrust into the patriarch role of the family, despite having her own serious health issues. And yet, never once did she complain or play the victim role. Instead, she traveled, kept up her friendships in Denver and in St. Pete, and enjoyed life as much as she could.

Now it's scene 1, take 2 all over again. The whole family is gathered around her. The hospice nurse is making my mom as comfortable as possible as she slowly slips into a comatose state. It's a movie my family has seen before and sadly we know how it's going to end.

The hospice nurse asks if it's okay if she sings to my mom. We all nod in approval, appreciating the uniqueness of the request. After a couple of hours, some of my siblings noticed a slight movement from my mom and call the rest of us over. Just then, my mom opened her eyes long enough to look around at all of us before closing her eyes and taking her last breath.

Like with my dad, I couldn't feel anything—until the realization hit that my siblings and I were parentless for the first time in our lives. The foundation that held our family together was now gone under the sheet that covered my mother's body. Suddenly, a haunting memory engulfed me from when I was a very young child. I had somehow gotten separated from my mom at a shopping mall and frantically called out her name out of sheer fear. This time she would never come back! I had lost her for good.

Aftermath

They say you can tell a lot about parents by how their kids turned out. I do think it fits in our case. I've never been so proud of my siblings, their spouses, their kids, and their kid's kids than I was during the ordeals described above. We all rallied for each other and for my parents during both their transitions and showed up like we've never shown up before. Even the process of dividing their possessions and closing out two homes was seamless. I know my parents would be proud of us, but it's really a testament to them and their everlasting legacy.

Rest in peace, Mary Lou and John Giesen! We'll see you in the next chapter.

25
The Solo Retreat

> *You have the answer.*
> *Just sit quiet enough to hear it.*
> — Pat Obuchowski

Every summer I gift myself a solo retreat at Chautauqua Park in Boulder, Colorado. This annual hermitage has been one of the best rituals I've created for myself and I'd like to tell you a little about it. For a change of pace, I'm going to tell this story as if you were interviewing me on this topic. Ready to play?

You: What exactly is a solo retreat?

Me: For me, a solo retreat is an opportunity to get away by myself where I can spend some uninterrupted reflection about both my personal life and work life in a meaningful way.

You: Why do you have to get away to do that?

Me: This kind of experience is much more powerful when there is an intentionality to it. Because I'm getting away for the sole purpose of self-reflection, it's much easier to focus on what I came there to do. It also helps going to a place where there are not a lot of distractions.

You: Is that why you like Chautauqua Park?

Me: Chautauqua Park is a community of cabins nestled against the Flatiron mountains. For a retreat location, it is ideal. The cabins have no TVs or radios and the community itself is very low key and peaceful. It's easy and comfortable to be alone, whether sitting on the porch or hiking the Flatirons.

You: How long are your solo retreats?

Me: I usually go for three or four days, but I mix in hikes and trips into town to add some variety.

You: That's a lot of time to be alone.

Me: That's the whole idea. I do my best thinking when I'm alone, relaxed, and not under a time crunch.

You: Tell me what do you do on these solo retreats?

Me: From a big picture perspective, I assess both my personal and work life over the past six months. I look at what worked, what didn't work, and what I need to change.

The front porch of my cabin where I spend the most time

You: How do you do that?

Me: I divide the retreat into three parts. The first part is simply reading my journal entries over the last six months. I'm a writer, so it shouldn't be a huge surprise that I journal.

You: What do you learn from reading your journal?

Me: Reading my journal provides a context for the past six months. It allows me to revisit all the highlights, lowlights, challenges, changes, and insights that I experienced from January to June. Without that part, I'd forget a lot of the things that happened, especially earlier in the year.

You: Okay, so what do you do next?

Me: Prior to the solo retreat, I create thought-provoking questions that I want to reflect on and address while at the retreat. This is the second part of the retreat and the most important. Typically, half of the questions are personal, and half are work related.

You: Can you give an example of some of these questions?

Me: Sure. Here are a few from the most recent retreat:

- What scares me the most about retiring early? What do I need to do to make that transition go as smoothly as possible?

- What personal relationships have meant the most to me over the past six months and why?

- What do I want my last six months at DU to be like? How do I make that happen?

- What were the moments over the past six months where I really felt alive? How do I create more of those going forward?

- What were the biggest challenges I faced recently, and what did I learn about myself in the process?

You: How many questions do you typically have to answer?

Me: I usually have about 15-to-20 total.

You: Okay, so you've read your journal and answered all of your questions. Then what?

Me: Then I'm ready for the third part, which is creating goals and an action plan for the next six months.

You: Why only 6 months?

Me: I think a year is too long. Too many things can change during a 12-month span.

You: Do you do another solo retreat in January?

Me: Sort of. I do a miniversion of this retreat around New Year's to update my goals and action items. I don't go on an actual retreat, per se, but I read my journal and answer open-ended questions at that time as well. It's just not as extensive as the summer solo retreat.

You: Does it have to be a solo retreat? I could see a benefit to doing this in tandem with a friend, spouse, or even business partner.

Me: It's possible to do this process with someone else, but you probably wouldn't get as much out of it. It's just adding another distraction, in my opinion. The whole idea of a solo retreat is to be alone and free of distractions. That's when the powerful insights happen.

You: Speaking about insights, have you had any "aha" moments from past retreats?

Me: I have them every year. Many have changed my life.

You: Can you share a recent one?

Me: During my 2017 solo retreat, I had an aha moment that it was time to move out of my home of 27 years. The thought of selling my house and moving was not even on my radar before the retreat. That was a big decision that I never saw coming.

You: Do you think you would have come to that decision eventually, without the retreat?

Me: I don't know. What I can tell you is that the retreat gave me the time to really think through a difficult situation that had occurred a couple months before. And because I had that quality time to reflect, the aha moment presented itself.

You: So, would you recommend these solo retreats to everyone?

Me: Yes, I would. There is tremendous benefit in getting away, having quality time alone, and doing self-reflection work. The retreat format can certainly be tweaked to accommodate each person, as long as those three components are present.

You: Any final thoughts?

Me: I just want to emphasize that a solo retreat is not a selfish endeavor. As I mentioned at the very beginning, the whole purpose of going on these retreats is for self-improvement. I always leave these retreats with a revitalized perspective, attitude, and focus. This not only benefits me, but all the people I come into contact with, personally or professionally. Everyone benefits! That's why the investment in time and money is worth every cent!

26
Are You a Giver or a Taker?

D o you give more than you take from others? Certainly, most of us would say that we give more, but do we? You might want to read this story before you answer.

The Workshop

Every time I entered the large hotel conference room, I wasn't sure what to expect. I was attending a three-day intensive program, and after every break the instructors would completely change up the room to accommodate the next experience. This time was no different. The room had been completely cleared out except for 95 chairs, neatly arranged in a large circle in the center of the room.

Now what are they going to make us do? I thought. I was still a little apprehensive about being at this personal development workshop.

The room felt cold as we were instructed to quickly take a seat. I looked around the circle, exchanging nervous nods to anyone that would look back. Within a couple of minutes every chair was filled. The doors slammed shut. It was exactly 2:00 p.m.

The lead trainer's voice bellowed over the sound system. "Please number off."

From across the circle I could hear the faint, "One . . . two . . . three," and so on until the ascending numbers came my way. "Sixty-two," I yelled, thankful I was still paying attention. Within a minute or so, all 95 of us had our numbers.

"Now take out a pen and pad of paper and divide your sheet into two columns. Label the first column *Giver* and the second column *Taker*."

The lead trainer continued. "All those with odd numbers will remain seated. Those with even numbers will stand and face the seated person to their right. For those of you standing, you are to look at the person seated in front of you and call out either giver or taker. There is to be no additional conversation. This needs to be done quickly. Then move to the right and do the same thing with the next seated person, and then the next, until you've made your way around the whole circle. Do you understand?"

We all nodded.

"What? I didn't hear you!" yelled the lead trainer.

A resounding *Yes!* filled the room.

"For those of you seated, keep a running count of your giver and taker scores. Once everyone standing has provided a rating for everyone seated, you will switch positions. Those seated will stand and those standing will be seated, and we will repeat the process. Is that clear?"

"Yes."

"Begin."

Before I could look up, a participant was standing in front of me, gazing at me with uncertainty. He paused.

"Let's go, let's go!" yelled a nearby assistant.

"Taker." His apologetic eyes moved to the next participant on my left.

Taker! I thought to myself. *Are you serious! I'm not a taker!*

A woman who I had briefly talked with earlier faced me next. "Taker."

OMG! What's going on here!

Then Jack, a member from my small group came through. *Surely, he'll give me a giver. He knows me, for Pete's sake!*

"Taker."

I gazed down at the floor in confusion. *What am I missing here!*

As each participant shuffled by, so did my distorted scores . . . *taker, taker, giver, taker, giver, taker, taker, taker* . . . and on it went.

By the end, I felt as if I'd been punched in the stomach. *How could people be so wrong about me!* I lamented. I knew I was a giver—or so I thought. Something was wrong. Why, even my small group—the group of people who I thought knew me—primarily scored me as a taker.

Just then the lead trainer's voice came over the sound system. "Now add up your scores in both columns." He paused. "Once you've done that, I'd like you to rearrange yourselves in the circle beginning with highest to lowest scores in the giver category. Quickly now!"

I could only shake my head. *Are you serious! I'm already humiliated internally and now I get to be humiliated in front of everybody. Can this workshop get any worse!*

The group moved in all directions as people frantically compared scores to find their spot. It had that organized chaos feeling of lining up for a Southwest flight; only this time I clearly wasn't going to be in the "A" or "B" group for boarding.

I gazed at my giver score of 33. A large gentleman was seated in the second-to-last seat, looking dejected. "What's your number?" I asked, trying to downplay this exercise.

"Twenty-eight," he replied. "You?"

"Thirty-three," I said in shame.

"You're next to me then," as he pointed to the seat on his left. "Welcome to the losers!"

To add insult to injury, just as everyone found their seats, the trainer entered the circle and asked us all to recite our giver scores to the whole group, beginning with the highest score on down to the lowest score.

At this point, the only thing that kept me from leaving was knowing that our small groups would be getting together again in a few minutes to process the exercise. As embarrassed as I was, I felt compelled to hear from my own teammates why they gave me the taker scores. I just needed to know. Besides, as I saw it, I already was at rock bottom on the humiliation scale, so the only place left to go was up!

The "Aha" Moment

I headed over to Breakout Room B where my group was assembling. I could hear loud talking and laughter as I entered, which surprised me a bit. *I'm so glad they are having such a good time at my expense,* I thought, as I took a seat at the conference table.

The topic of conversation shifted over to the exercise. As group members shared their experiences, the energy in the room was booming, which made my sullen disposition stand out even more. I've never been very good at masking my feelings, and this was no exception. I was confused, shook up, and a little angry with the group.

Suddenly the room became quiet—too quiet. I looked up only to see five pairs of concerned eyes looking right at me.

"Are you okay?" asked Kathy.

"Not really."

"What's going on?" she asked softly.

The rest of the group leaned in to hear my response.

"I was humiliated out there, that's what!" I said. "Everybody, including most of you, called me a taker."

Jack jumped in. "Greg, I don't think you are a taker. In fact, I know you're not."

"Then why did you say taker?" I asked.

"It had nothing to do with who you are or our relationship. It was all about how you were showing up in the moment."

I was confused. "What moment?"

"The moment when I was standing in front of you. That moment."

Heads were nodding around the table.

Jack continued. "Dude, you looked scared sitting there in that chair, like you were expecting something bad to happen. Does that make sense?" he asked.

Before I could respond, Janice stepped into the conversation. "For me it was based on how I was feeling in your presence—and truthfully, I was having trouble connecting to you. Believe me, I wanted to say giver so bad, but I wasn't feeling it."

"What was I doing that said taker?" I asked.

"It was what you weren't doing," replied Tom, another member. "The people that were smiling and radiating love while sitting there were the people who I gave giver scores to. When I got to you," as he paused to search for the right words, "I didn't get anything back. I don't know if that makes any sense, but you weren't giving me anything. It felt like you were taking."

Just then it started to make sense. I jumped up. "What you're saying is, you weren't judging me as a person, but responding to my body language in that moment?"

Everyone in the group simultaneously nodded. "Exactly."

I could feel a lightness come over me. "I think I'm getting it. Instead of embracing the moment and welcoming each person that stood in front of me, I braced myself for the worst."

"Yes, yes, yes!" yelled Jack. "You got it!"

I was smiling now as I looked at the group. "This was powerful. Thank you!"

"Say more?" asked Kathy. "What was powerful?"

"The insight you all just gave me about myself." I replied. "I've been responding and reacting to life instead of simply welcoming it. Just like in that exercise, I was guarded, apprehensive, and in self-protective mode." My voice started to crack as my emotions took over. "I didn't realize it . . . until now."

"So, what are you going to do differently?" asked Janice.

"I'm going to embrace all of my experiences, both good and bad. I'm going to welcome people into my life instead of holding back. I'm going to get out of my head and reveal my true self more."

As I glanced around the room, everyone was smiling at me. Tom was the first to come over and hug me, followed by the rest of the group. It was of those rare moments in time when I could literally feel the love in the room.

"I told you," said Jack, as we headed out of the room after the lovefest ended.

"You told me what?"

"That you were a giver. You made that happen," as he pointed over to Breakout Room B.

I smiled. "I told you I was a giver!"

27
The "Greater Yes"

When you are interested, you do it when
it is convenient. When you are committed,
you accept no excuses, only results.

— Ken Blanchard

A few years ago, I joined six other business owners from across the country to be a part of a mastermind group. The purpose of this mastermind group was to provide coaching and support to each other around our individual business goals, thus creating greater accountability and results for each of us. In order to do this, we agreed to fully participate in biweekly conference calls, plus attend quarterly retreats where we would all get together in person for more in-depth information sharing and coaching. We also created group norms around things like punctuality, meeting behavior, and performance expectations. The group was very serious about its purpose and the commitment level that was required.

Or so I thought.

During my first conference call, one of our members could be heard typing away on his computer throughout the session.

Although that behavior might not be unusual in some settings, it broke our norm to turn off all electronic distractions during our calls so we could be fully present with each other. Since I was the newest member, I didn't say anything, even though I found the typing to be a bit distracting.

At the end of the meeting, Sondra, our organizer and group leader, spoke up. "Michael, may I ask you what you were doing typing during our meeting?"

Defensively, Michael shot back. "I had no choice, there were a couple pressing emails I had to get out."

"The reason we created group norms, like no electronics, was so that we could be fully present with one another. You agreed to those norms and yet disregarded them," she pressed.

"Well," he replied firmly, "It was either miss this conference call or get those emails out, Sondra. Sometimes norms have to be broken."

"What's the point of having group norms if we are not going to follow them," said Sondra. She invited the rest of us to chime in.

Before others could speak, Michael continued his assault. "These rules are childish. They need to be suggested guidelines and nothing more!"

Just then, other members spoke up, siding with either Michael or Sondra. Within seconds, people were raising their voices, in an effort to be heard. Chaos ensued, like the freefall of a rollercoaster on its way down the tracks. Things got totally out of control, and the conference call ended.

The next morning, Michael resigned from the group. An hour later, Marilyn resigned, followed by Thomas. Just like that, we were down to four, and I hadn't yet fully committed to being in the group.

Later that morning, Mark, my buddy who brought me into the mastermind group, called to check in. "Dude, I don't know what to say. I'm sorry you had to witness all of that on your first call."

"Is that how they all go?" I questioned.

"No, of course not. Tension had been mounting between Michael and Sondra and everything hit the fan yesterday. How are you doing with all of it?" Before letting me respond, he added, "Obviously the group is falling apart. This would be the time to bail, if you want to quit."

I must admit, I was relieved to know that I had an out. My first and only conference call with this group had been an uncomfortable experience, even though I was primarily a bystander. "I'm not sure." I replied. "What are you going to do?"

"I think I'll stay," he said. "Seven seemed like too many people anyway."

Before responding, I reflected on why I wanted to join this mastermind group in the first place. I recalled the excitement of having my own business advisors; people I could really talk to about my company, my clients, and my services. I also liked the support and accountability that framed the purpose of this group. *Where else you going to get that?* I thought. But to be in a group like this required a commitment that included adhering to the group norms, something that Michael, Marilyn, and Thomas were unwilling to do.

My Mastermind Group, a.k.a. G-7

"You know what, Mark," I said with conviction, "I'm totally in! It was never about the size of the group for me, it's always been about the purpose and the commitment to each other. Yes, let's do this."

So we did. Our mastermind group lasted for three years and was one of the most powerful experiences and fondest memories of my business life.

The "Greater Yes!"

The mastermind story demonstrates what I call the "greater yes." The greater yes is an unyielding commitment to something or someone that is so compelling that it will override any adversity or challenge. For me, the benefits of staying in the group far outweighed any of the negative aspects, such as the tight structure of the meetings. In short, I wanted to learn what this group had to offer, and I was willing to give up some freedom to make that happen. That was my greater yes.

Often, we commit to something without identifying our greater yes. In that case, we haven't committed at all. That was the case with Michael, Marilyn, and Thomas. They wanted to be in the group as long as it was convenient and met their immediate needs. But the moment their commitment was put to the test, they bailed; not because they couldn't gain anything from the group, but because they weren't willing to abide by the ground rules that they agreed to follow. In other words, they didn't have a greater yes.

Signs when we are missing a greater yes:

- We're easy-going, yet hesitant to get overly involved in something.

- If we're not feeling it, we're not doing it.

- Our actions don't match up with our words.

- We always have one foot out the door, ready to abort on a moment's notice.

- We find ourselves going through the motions, but not sure why.

- We'll commit to something—until something better comes along.

- We have a "wait-and-see" attitude about everything.

- We're not quite sure what we want, so anything will do—at least for now.

- We'll let external circumstances dictate our decisions.

- We have a hard time looking someone in the eye to say, "Yes I will!"

The greater yes reveals our passion, purpose, and desire. We don't wonder "if" something is going to happen but "when" it's going to happen. We have confidence that we will achieve something, even if we don't know exactly how.

Signs when we have a greater yes:

- We know what we want.

- We are willing to do whatever it takes to make something happen.

- We view adversity and challenges as merely obstacles to get around.

- If at first we don't succeed, we try a different approach.

- If we're not feeling something wholeheartedly, we try it anyway.

- Our word is our commitment.

- We make things happen instead of waiting for things to happen.

- We look people in the eye and say, "Yes I will."

- If we don't like something, we either change it or find a way to embrace it.

Having a greater yes begins when we know what we want and why we want it. Add a little passion and determination to the mix, and you've got your greater yes.

This book is filled with stories that required me to have a greater yes. That's why I could overcome many of the challenges I faced. Even writing these stories and publishing this book are proof of my greater yes. I never questioned whether it would get finished. I always knew it would, one way or another.

So, the next time you are questioning your level of commitment to something, ask yourself what is the greater yes? If it exists, identify it, embrace it, and make the thing happen. If it doesn't exist, move on to something else. It's not worth your time.

28
The Puppeteer

*You can learn more about a person in one hour
of play than a lifetime of conversation.*

— Plato

'vе never acted in a play or been a part of a the-
ater production of any kind. I can't sing, dance,
or play a musical instrument. I'm shy, quiet, and introverted. Not
exactly thespian characteristics.

Fortunately, I was naïve enough to give puppeteering a try.

It was the spring of 1997 when I visited the website of the
local Renaissance Festival. I intended to purchase some discounted
tickets for the upcoming summer season when an audition ad
popped up. There was a list of all the vacant roles they needed to
fill, so I scrolled through, as much out of boredom as curiosity.
A photo of a very large puppet came on the screen with the title,
"Puppeteer Needed."

It caught my eye. *A puppeteer? How fun would that be to simply
walk around without having to act or perform or even talk, and still be
the center of attention! I could do that.*

The Queen puppet with the King right behind her

I didn't think that there was much more to being a puppeteer and a member of the Renaissance Festival cast than what the photo depicted. So I made the call and added my name to the auditions.

The Auditions

As I drove to the University of Denver, where the tryouts were happening, I wondered what I would be asked to do. *It couldn't be much of anything,* I thought, *probably a coordination test of some sort inside the puppet outfit. Either way, it shouldn't be too difficult.*

Once on campus, I was stunned by the number of crazy characters who were all walking over to the Mary Reed Building. Everyone was dressed in Renaissance-era costumes, and most were speaking with English dialect.

Guess I didn't get the memo, I thought, feeling totally out of place in my blue jeans and T-shirt. Inside the building, I saw a crowd of knights, maidens, lords, ladies, peasants, pirates, beggars, belly dancers, and, of course a king and queen, all greeting and hugging each other as if they were old friends at a high school reunion.

I looked around for a familiar face or possibly a sign on the wall for puppeteers, but I found no clues. I was either going to have to figure it out by myself, or locate an escape route.

Moments later the loudspeaker came on.

"Welcome, thespians," shouted Anna, the Renaissance director. "I hope you all had a fantastic winter break. As most of you know, we will be rehearsing every Saturday from now until June 1st, when we open the gates for our season debut. Please organize yourselves into groups of six people and spread out. A team member will be working with you for the morning."

Before I could move, five others had circled around me to form a group. Richard, one of the team members, joined us and introduced himself. When he got to me, I asked about the puppeteer audition.

He smiled. "That comes much later on. We're here to practice our acting."

"Wait, what?" I cried. "I'm just doing the puppet, not the acting. You know, those big puppets?"

Richard put his arm around me. "All puppeteers need to create a second character so they can be out with our patrons when they are not in the puppet suit. So, guess what? You will be acting."

"Seriously?" I asked.

Ignoring me, he began explaining the improv activity we were about to do as a group. It was a storytelling exercise where one person starts a story and the next person continues it and so on until the whole group has contributed. It's pretty funny to watch, but I was still absorbing the fact that I had to create a second character. *That's not what I signed up for!*

The improv activities took up most of the morning—the longest and most uncomfortable two hours of my life—and culminated with another surprise. We gathered into one large group facing the King and Queen and were told to formally present ourselves, one at a time, to the royal couple. We were to use proper English etiquette and accent, and introduce our character by name.

I had nothing.

Call it the beginning of the end or the tipping point of the morning, but I was done! I had no intention of acting, creating a second character, or learning to speak with an English accent. Nope. It wasn't going to happen. And I certainly wasn't going to embarrass myself in front of the King and Queen.

I surveyed the room and planned my escape. I crouched down a bit and tiptoed down the corridor, hoping not to attract attention. As I reached the door, a loud voice bellowed out for all to hear.

"Where are you going, Greg Giesen?"

Everybody looked in my direction. Anna, the director, spotted me by the door and clearly knew my name.

"Excuse me?" I replied sheepishly, like a little kid caught stealing.

"We need you down here," she stated in no uncertain terms.

With everyone staring, I caved. "Okay."

I walked right up to the King and Queen, and with no idea of proper etiquette, no English accent, and no character in mind, I simply said, "I'm Greg."

Everyone laughed.

Then two or three people stepped up to show me how to bow and what to say. They didn't care if I had a character or not, they just wanted to help.

I was surprised. Even though I had made myself an "outcast," people still jumped in to help me. Maybe there was a way to make this work after all.

The Second Rehearsal and Beyond

If not for the kindness shown to me at the first rehearsal, this story would have ended there. Instead, I changed my attitude. I tried again.

I accepted the fact that I needed a second character. I also knew that the improv exercises were helping me with my confidence and acting skills. And I was slowly bonding with other cast members and feeling more and more included. But the biggest thing I realized was that I needed to make a commitment to the Renaissance Festival, to my fellow cast members, to Anna, and to myself, in order for this to work. I couldn't go in half-assed. Not if I wanted to get something real out of this experience.

So, I did!

For eight weekends that summer, I was a puppeteer and a henchman (my second character). As I write this, I'm still surprised at how much I embraced both roles and how much I stepped out of my comfort zone.

My favorite part of being inside the giant puppet was dancing to the beat of the drumming circle, held every Saturday and Sunday afternoon in the open square. I felt like a little kid without inhibitions, as I danced and entertained patrons of all ages. Have you ever seen one of those big puppets dance? It's quite the sight.

As the henchman, I would jump up on a large boulder and solicit volunteers for the afternoon hangings, using my best English dialect. To participate in these fictitious hangings, I sold personalized death certificates for a couple dollars. It became a popular gimmick, and I made a few bucks as well.

By summer's end, I had gained so much more from this experience than I ever imagined. I got to play like a kid again and be a puppeteer. I was able to experience the Renaissance Festival from the inside-out. I entertained people. I stepped out of my comfort zone. And I got to meet and hang out with an incredible group of cast members.

But most importantly, I proved to myself that I can do anything and be anything if I'm willing to stick with it.

Not too bad for a summer gig!

29
Let Go of My Ego

*This isn't a book of what I know . . .
it's what I'm trying to learn.*

— John Heider

A number of years ago, I participated in a 270-hour facilitator training that was based on the book, *The Tao of Leadership* by John Heider. What really attracted me to this course were both the experiential format and the intensive weekend retreats each month, culminating in a final weekend when the master facilitator and author would join us.

To give a little perspective, when I took this nine-month course, I was a different person. It was early in my career and I was trying to prove to myself and to my profession that I was worthy, competent, and qualified. For me that meant being well-versed in all the latest and greatest concepts, theories, books, and models I could get my hands on. I attended conferences, joined professional associations, wrote articles, and got certified in every assessment imaginable. I was trying to project an image of competence and success to others. What I really needed, however, was to convince myself.

As the course got underway, it immediately felt different from other courses I had taken. First, instead of being held in a classroom setting, it took place in a group therapy room in a converted old house. And instead of chairs or tables, we sat on the floor with pillows. Did I mention the meditation music and incense? Yep, we had that too. But probably the biggest surprise for me was the realization that we were to be not only students, but also subjects as well. We'd be practicing our facilitation skills on each other, in front of the whole group, and then we would receive feedback from the instructors and the group on how we did.

Perhaps it was performance anxiety or nervousness or perfectionism—or maybe all three—that prevented me from fully engaging and volunteering for the facilitator role whenever the option was offered. I took copious notes when someone else facilitated, but I never felt competent enough to put myself out there, let alone open myself up for feedback. I just couldn't do it. Too much to learn, too many notes to go through, and frankly, I just wasn't comfortable. In hindsight, I think much of my anxiety came from watching how flawlessly the instructors seemed to be when they were demonstrating for us. It was like watching an artist transform an empty canvas into a work of art. *There's no way I could do that without notes, a teleprompter, and a prayer,* I'd say to myself.

As the months went by, opportunities passed for me to facilitate in front of the group. Everything I had learned was in my head at this point, but I was unable to put it into practice. Then the John Heider weekend came—and everything changed.

I had never met John Heider before, but I had created an image of him in my mind based on his book, his work, and the admiration that the instructors had for him. I recall imagining a deity-like figure with long hair and a beard, dressed in a flowing robe—you get the idea. As silly as that sounds, you can imagine my surprise when the actual man emerged from a beat-up Toyota Celica. I saw a slightly out-of-shape person wearing a T-shirt and wrinkled pants—and smoking a cigarette! Instead of coming right in, he stood outside his car and finished off his smoke. When he finally came in, the instructors greeted him and introduced him to the whole group.

My first real impression of John changed the moment I shook hands with him. He was a very large man, with a gentle gaze and a big smile. His eyes radiated love, making me want to tell him my whole life story in an instant. His subtle charisma was so welcoming and safe.

Once in the group room, John planted himself in the middle of floor, looking like an American version of Buddha. He smiled and gazed around the circle, bypassing any formalities or introduction, and said, "Who'd like to work with me?"

Immediately Tamara raised her hand and joined him in the center of the circle.

I pulled out my notepad and pen, ready to record everything.

"Tell me what you want me to know," he says.

Tamara seemed to be struggling with her words, unable to talk.

John continued to smile, making her feel like the most important person in the universe. He was in no hurry and willing to wait. He was as present as a person could be with another.

Tamara started to cry.

John leaned in gently and asked her what the tears were about.

"I'm so sad," she said. "My husband left me and I'm not sure what I'm going to do."

"I can see you are hurting," he said. "Tell me more."

She proceeded to explain the fight she and her husband had that led to the ensuing break-up. Her tears kept flowing. John stayed right there with her in the most caring way, yet without consoling her.

He leaned in again. "Can you point to the part of your body that is hurting the most right now?"

She touched her stomach.

At this point, something transformational was not only happening between John and Tamara, but for me as well. Without noticing, I had put my pen and paper down, and for the first time in this program, I was completely present with what was happening in front of me.

John, still smiling, asked, "If your tummy could talk right now, what would it want to say?"

Immediately my eyebrows raised up. *Tummy? Are you serious! This guy's a master!*

Seconds later Tamara began talking and opening up. John then skillfully facilitated a dialogue between her tummy and her heart. I couldn't believe what I was seeing—and it was working! Within the next 10 minutes Tamara worked through her intense emotions and was smiling and radiating positive energy.

"How did you know what to do next?" someone asked John afterward.

"I didn't," he responded. "I just stayed present with her and created the container for her to do her own work. My questions merely came from a place of curiosity. You need to remember it's not about directing someone's process; it's about being with their process. It's about creating a space for them to guide themselves. When you are thinking about what to do next or where to go, you are back in your head and you've made it about you. Facilitation isn't about you—it's about them. How can you be present with another if you are thinking about what to do or how to do it? All the information you need is right in front of you. Pay attention."

I couldn't believe what I was hearing. It was like he was talking directly to me.

He went on to say, "You need to learn whatever you need to learn and then let it go. You can't bring your notes, your books, or your ego in with you when you are working with someone. You simply bring yourself, your love, and your curiosity."

I jumped in, "But what if you don't know what to do?"

"Again, that would be about you. It's not about you."

"Okay," I said, "so what do you do when you don't know what to do?"

He smiled. "I let the client guide the conversation. I ask questions. I don't push, I don't pull, I simply hold a safe and loving space for them. Trust the process!"

At that moment it all sunk in. I thought I needed to be the expert. I thought I needed to have the answers. I thought the success or failure of a facilitated conversation was on my shoulders. It's no wonder I was having such a hard time facilitating. I had put all of the burden on me.

At that moment, with John Heider, I became a facilitator. Granted, it took me until the final weekend of a nine-month course to get there, but it was well worth it.

Afterward

I was facilitating a problem-solving session with a corporate team when they got stuck. With all eyes looking at me to help them get unstuck, I said to the group, "Looks like you're stuck right now. What do you need to do to get past this?"

After a minute of awkwardness, one member threw out a suggestion which led to another member's suggestion. Before they knew it, the group was off and running again. At the end of the session, the group was happy with their work and high-fiving each other as they left the room.

I smiled, knowing how proud John would have been with my facilitation.

Before leaving, I sat down for a second and looked up to the heavens and thanked John for everything he did for me that day back in facilitator training. *I couldn't have done it without you, old man!*

As I turned out the lights and headed home, I recalled the inscription John had written in my copy of *The Tao of Leadership*. It said, "To Greg. Just Do It!"

Talk about hitting the nail on the head.

Rest in peace, John Heider!

30
The Vulnerability Trap

> *What lies behind us, and what lies before us are small matters compared to what lies within us.*
>
> — Ralph Waldo Emerson

Jeffrey had a lot of influence within the group, but not necessarily in a good way. On the surface, he had it all going on. He was athletic, good looking, and very experienced in the outdoors education environment. Every activity we did during the first two days of the program, he had probably done a hundred times before. At least that's what he said. When we had to climb the 35-foot power pole and jump off from the top, Jeffrey climbed blindfolded. He said it was just too easy for him otherwise.

But while Jeffrey excelled in the activities, he also managed to alienate his teammates in the process. These first two days were supposed to help us bond and become a team. We were about to go into the wilderness together for eight days, and we needed to be able to count on each other. But for Jeffrey, it was all about Jeffrey. He clearly enjoyed having an advantage over the rest of us, and he made sure we all knew it. To show off his superiority, he always had to go first in every activity. Then he would sit back and enjoy watching the rest of us flounder.

On the second day, we had one final activity to do before dinner and packing up for our excursion. By this point, we had all gotten used to Jeffrey's grandiose ways. And, in a weird sort of way, he actually brought the rest of us together.

Patrick, our lead instructor, gathered us together. "This is called *Wind in the Willows,*" he said. "It's a trust exercise where each of you will get a chance to be in the center of the circle with your eyes closed. You will then fall back into the waiting hands of your teammates who will gently move you around the circle—back and forth and to the side."

While Patrick demonstrated the correct body posture for both being in the center and for supporting the person in the center, many of us smiled and looked around. Collectively, we wondered, *How will Jeffrey hijack this one?*

"So, who'd like to go first?" Patrick asked.

Dead silence.

We all glanced around with our eyebrows raised. You know how groundhogs' heads pop up from the ground all at once? That's kind of what we looked like at that moment.

More dead silence.

"Look, guys," said Patrick, "we need to get going."

Finally, someone other than Jeffrey volunteered.

Perhaps being a team player is finally sinking in, I thought, as I glanced over toward Jeffrey and smiled. But nothing . . . no reaction.

More and more of the group members took their turn, but still no Jeffrey.

"Jeffrey," called Patrick, "you're the last one."

Something clearly was wrong. From a trust-building perspective, this activity wasn't nearly as difficult as the power pole challenge, and yet Jeffrey looked timid. What happened to his "Anything you can do, I can do better" attitude, I wondered.

Waving his hand to signal *No thanks*, Jeffrey responded, "Been there, done that."

"I don't care," shouted Patrick, getting annoyed, "we are all doing it."

"Seriously," complained Jeffrey, "I've done this a hundred times. I'm gonna skip it."

The two squared off while we all watched.

"Listen to me," said Patrick. "We've got things to do and we cannot move on until you get your rear end in the circle."

Jeffrey slowly and reluctantly headed toward the center of the circle.

Crystal, a fellow participant, touched Jeffrey's shoulder to let him know it was going to be okay.

He jumped, like he had just seen a ghost.

"Sorry, I was just trying to help," apologized Crystal.

Sweat was now dripping from Jeffrey's brow.

"Get into position," directed Patrick.

Jeffrey was noticeably shaking, hesitant to close his eyes.

Patrick changed his tone, now seeing the fear that took over. "Look at me Jeffrey, what's going on?"

Jeffrey stiffened up. "Nothing, I'm fine."

He took a big breath before attempting to fall back. He was literally shaking. He stopped himself. He regrouped and tried a second time but still couldn't commit to falling back. Finally, by the third attempt, he slowly leaned back far enough to come into contact with our hands ready to support him. But instead of easing into our hands, he bent over in the opposite direction and crashed to the ground.

He covered his face as his body shook. He was crying.

"Are you okay?" cried Kelly, while Kimberly stroked his back with her hand.

"Let him be," asserted Patrick, "and give him some space."

All eyes were glued on Jeffrey. We were as scared as he was.

I must admit, for a guy who triggered me so, I never felt more care and compassion for him than I did at that moment; and it wasn't just me. Our whole team rallied around him. It was exactly what we needed. Jeffrey's vulnerability literally brought the whole group together for the first time.

But it was short-lived.

Within seconds, Jeffrey brushed himself off, apologized for having been weak, and went right back to being the jerk that we all became accustomed to seeing. His brief instance of true authenticity was merely an aberration for him. He saw it as weakness; a mistake; a moment to forget. He just couldn't get out of his own way.

Rarely will these types of outdoor education programs release a participant; but Jeffrey was kicked out four days later for continually refusing to be a team player. Ultimately, he put our group in jeopardy when he separated himself from us on the climb down Mount Elbert, choosing instead to go on his own. Unfortunately for Jeffrey, the instructors had enough of his antics and escorted him off the mountain and out of the program later that night.

Although Jeffrey never understood the importance of team dynamics, he did a pretty good job of teaching it to the rest of us. I guess there are no accidents!

31
A Runner's Hi

> *To be beautiful means to be yourself. You don't need to*
> *be accepted by others. You need to accept yourself.*
>
> — Thich Nhat Hanh

I was out running on the trails near Denver one warm and sunny Saturday morning. I was feeling good, both physically and mentally. As I looked down the path ahead of me, I noticed another runner coming toward me. As he came upon me, I looked into his eyes and acknowledged him with a nod (a common gesture among runners), but the man ignored me. He passed with a scowl on his face.

I wondered why people seem to be less and less friendly these days. *Isn't returning an acknowledgment the polite thing to do? I mean, really, how much effort does it take to at least nod back?* I thought.

As I ran, I continued to think about the man with the scowl. After a few minutes, I concluded that I'll only disappoint myself if I keep expecting something in return when I initiate a greeting with a passing runner. In fact, why even waste my time?

Moments later, I spotted another runner coming toward me on the path. Still bugged from the unfriendliness of the last one, I decided to keep my eyes toward the ground, avoiding any kind of greeting with her. Then, just as our paths crossed, I heard a very friendly "Hi" and caught a welcoming smile as she passed by me. I called out a belated "Hi," but she was already too far away to hear it.

Just then it hit me. I had allowed the first runner to dictate my attitude toward the next one. I had allowed my friendliness to be conditional! Yikes! That's not the person I want to be.

I then asked myself if I could simply acknowledge other runners without expecting something in return? Could I just be friendly because that is who I am—period?

The answer was a resounding YES!

Being authentic is what I'm all about. That means being true to myself and showing up that way, regardless of how others may or may not react.

Such a simple example. Such a profound reminder.

32
The Things We Think but Do Not Say!

> Too often we underestimate the power of a touch,
> a smile, a kind word, a listening ear, an honest
> compliment, or the smallest act of caring, all of
> which have the potential to turn a life around.
>
> — Leo Buscaglia

Why do we hold back on saying the things that matter?

In the movie *Jerry Maguire*, Jerry, played by Tom Cruise, has an epiphany in the middle of the night that ends up changing his life. In that moment he comes to the realization that his agency's focus on getting more clients is completely wrong. *Instead*, he asserts, *the focus needs to be put on the relationship with our current clients by providing more time, attention, and caring.*

Jerry's passion for change served him well by the end of the movie, although, initially, his company pushes him out for his radical ideas. But isn't it always a risk to say what we really feel? After all, honesty can be a game changer when it comes to relationships.

One of my coaching clients was pressured to leave his position and finally decided to take another job instead of facing a slow and painful death. Despite being happy to be free of a miserable situation, he had mixed feelings about whether or not he was leaving on his own terms. Was he? I guess you could spin it either way.

What was interesting, however, was what he said in our last coaching session together. He told me how surprised he was to receive so many heartfelt comments from his staff, his peers, and his superiors during his final week. They all made a point to say goodbye.

"What do you mean?" I said.

He shook his head. "If people really felt that way about me, then why did they wait until I was leaving to tell me? I had the impression everyone wanted me out."

I had no answer.

I come from a very loving family, although our love is more implied than verbally stated. In fact, the first time I actually told my father I loved him was just hours before he passed away in his hospital bed. It seemed so easy to say it at that moment—and yet so difficult to say it before then.

What is it about endings that makes it easier to be authentic, honest, and loving with the people who are leaving us? And why can't we be that authentic, honest, and loving all along with the people in our lives?

Many companies ask departing employees to give an "exit interview" with Human Resources. The hope is that employees will be brutally honest about their experience at the company and provide some useful feedback for the future. Sounds reasonable, right? Yet few people find that process safe. One coaching client told me that he decided to forgo his exit interview because he didn't want to burn any bridges in the field. What's ironic is that the reason he left was because of the dysfunctional way business was being handled. Still, he chose to remain silent.

Isn't open and honest communication a fundamental expectation in any relationship, whether work or personal? Why are there so many exceptions to the rule?

When I've designed and facilitated team-building sessions for intact groups, my goal is typically to create enough trust so that open and honest communication could follow. I've discovered that it can take the better part of a day before a group feels comfortable enough to provide useful feedback to one another or to discuss sensitive issues. And these are groups that work with each other every day.

Stealing from the *Jerry Maguire* movie, we would end our Leading From Within workshop *(a 3-day program on authentic leadership)* with an activity called, *The Things We Think But Do Not Say.* That exercise provided the opportunity for participants to acknowledge each other for something significant they said or did during the workshop. Because this activity comes near the end of the program, the comments are always heartfelt and often very emotional.

Bottom Line

Why do endings give us the courage to say the things we think but do not say? Is it because it's our last chance? Is it because it takes time to become honest, transparent, and vulnerable with others? I'm not sure, but I wish there were more Jerry Maguires out there. I wish we didn't have to wait until someone was leaving before telling them how much they mean to us. I wish at work we could say what we mean without it feeling awkward or uncomfortable. I wish honesty and open communication were more the norm instead of the exception to the rule.

Perhaps instead of wishing so much, I should focus on doing it more myself.

33

I Thought I Lost Him

*Someone asked me what's the most difficult thing
about owning a dog. I replied, "The goodbye."*

— Stephan Pastis

This is the story about my relationship with my dog, Bailey. In many ways he was, and always will be, my best friend, treating me with unconditional love for more than 15 years. Over those years we went through many ups and downs, but nothing could prepare me for what took place on March 27, 2017, the day I thought I lost him for good.

The Backstory

I got Bailey when he was six months old. I was exercising at our neighborhood Rec Center when I came across a For Sale ad on the community bulletin board with a picture of Bailey. It was the cutest photo I'd ever seen of a Yorkie puppy, playfully staring back at me. Since my wife and I had decided it was time to get a second dog, I impulsively pulled out my cell phone and called the number listed, hoping I was the first to see the ad.

"Hi. I'm calling about the Yorkie for sale."

"You are the first to call. He's $500," said the lady.

"I'll take him."

"Do you have another dog?" she asked.

"Yes, we have a two-year-old Italian Greyhound named Lucky. Why?"

"Can you bring Lucky with you when you come over? We want to make sure the dogs are compatible."

"Of course," I said. At this point I would have agreed to anything just to close the deal. Her phone kept beeping from other calls during our conversation. At one point she put me on hold to answer.

"You're sure popular today," I said.

"Bailey's the popular one," she said. "The calls haven't stopped."

I smiled at my good fortune. *Perhaps Bailey and I were meant to be together!*

To no surprise, Bailey and Lucky hit it off immediately, with Bailey assuming the alpha role the moment he walked into our home. Lucky was a very passive dog and was just happy to have a playmate. As Bailey settled in to his new life, his attachment to me as his primary caretaker grew stronger by the day. Before long he was following me around the house from room to room, demanding to get up on my lap whenever I sat in the recliner. He'd even try to slip out the door whenever I had to leave, in hopes I'd take him

Bailey (on the right) waiting for me to throw his ball

with me. It became a battle of wits just to get out of the house on the mornings I had to see clients.

One of the best parts of having a dog is the unconditional love and reception you get when you come home after a long day of work. Lucky and Bailey were no exception. They would both go crazy in their own way. Lucky would run right at me and jump up and down. Bailey, on the other hand, would scramble to get one of his miniature tennis balls before running over and barking through the ball that he held tightly in his mouth. I came to love that muffled bark.

All Good Things Must Come to an End

My wife and I never had kids, so Lucky and Bailey were it. They were as spoiled as dogs could be. They had a nice fenced-in backyard, a doggy door from the kitchen to the yard, and unlimited access to the living room couches. They even slept with us—actually, between us—during the night. Neither one of us had the heart to boot them out of our bed. We found it easier to just embrace our new routine.

Looking back, I have such fond memories of those years as a pseudo-family—but it wasn't meant to be. After eight years, my wife and I decided to call it quits. She moved back into her condo that she'd been leasing, and I kept the house. That was the easy part of the decision. Much harder was letting Lucky go. Since he was the barker between the two, I thought he would provide added security for her at the condo. Had I known that I was never going to see him again, I would have argued to keep both dogs.

What surprised me more than the divorce or the emptiness of the house was my attachment to Bailey. I felt an obligation to be with him as much as possible, in order to fill the void left by Lucky and my wife. I found myself ending social evenings early so I could be home to feed him and hang out. I started bringing

Bailey's favorite place to rest at work . . . out in the hallway

him with me to appointments, family gatherings, and even to my weekly radio show. We were becoming inseparable.

At about that time, I accepted a full-time job at the University of Denver. This was an opportunity of a lifetime for me, although it meant being away from the house and Bailey a lot more. But as my first year at DU progressed, I started experimenting by bringing Bailey in with me a couple days a month, just to see how he'd handle being around a busy office. I also wondered how my colleagues would respond to having him there. To my surprise, it was a match made in heaven. My colleagues loved Bailey and he loved being the center of attention. It seemed that he was more popular with the DU community than I ever was! Go figure. Soon, a couple days a month turned into a couple days a week.

The Surprise Attack

My neighbors had two large dogs, both under three years old and full of energy. The decaying fence that separated our backyards had slats with enough space between them that our dogs could see each other and even greet each other from time to time. As a dog lover, I made a point to get to know my neighbor's dogs by name. I would pet them over the fence on a regular basis. Bailey, on the other hand, mostly ignored them, probably because they were too big and too rough for his little stature.

One Monday afternoon in March, a couple of years ago, I arrived at home, listening to my usual sports radio show as I hit the garage door opener. Once the door lifted, I could hear Bailey in the background barking and running around the house, like he always does when he knows I'm home. Although I usually come right in, I wanted to hear the end of the program and decided to stay in my car and listen for another minute or two. Meanwhile, Bailey moved outside and over to the side of the house, closest to the garage. He was barking with the ball in his mouth, excited as usual to see me.

Finally, the segment ended, and I got out of my car, but not before I heard a loud scream from the backyard. *Wait, did that come from my backyard?* The scream sounded like a baby's cry when something terribly wrong has happened. My heart raced. I listened for more but heard nothing. Since my neighbor's wife runs a daycare with very young children, I figured it had to have come from my neighbor's backyard, not mine. Still, it was a disturbing sound, and I had to check it out. Something wasn't feeling right!

I entered the house, expecting to see Bailey, but instead was greeted by both of my neighbor's dogs. They had somehow managed to fit through Bailey's doggy door, wagging their tails and jumping up on me. This was so wrong on so many levels! *What are they doing in my house? How did they get in my backyard? And where's Bailey!*

I dashed through the kitchen and out the sliding glass door, frantically calling out Bailey's name. "Bailey, Bailey, where are you boy?"

I braced myself as I rounded the corner to the side of the house. There, lying in a puddle of blood, was Bailey, gasping for air, with large bite marks around his little body and around his neck. He looked like he was dying.

I screamed at the two retreating dogs, "What did you do to him!" and knelt down and carefully lifted Bailey into my arms. The two dogs slipped between the broken slats and back into their yard.

Barely breathing and clearly in shock, Bailey was as limp as could be. I frantically put him in the backseat of my car and headed to the only animal hospital I could remember, at least 20 minutes away. I quickly called my neighbor's wife.

"Bailey was attacked by your dogs!"

"Is this Greg? What are you talking about?"

"Your dogs got through the fence and attacked Bailey. He's bleeding all over from bite marks and I'm taking him to an animal hospital. I don't know if he's going to make it!"

"I'll tell Shawn. I'm so sorry."

Between cursing the bumper-to-bumper traffic and pleading with Bailey not to die, I finally made it to the animal hospital and rushed him in. Fortunately, things were a little slow and they took him immediately into surgery.

I sat down in the waiting room, completely wiped out physically and emotionally. It was surreal. One moment I was casually listening to sports radio, and the next moment I was racing to the animal hospital to save Bailey's life. Meanwhile, I knew I had no control over how this story was going to end. I could only pray that Bailey would be given a second chance.

About an hour-and-a-half later, the surgeon came out to talk with me. I studied his face as he approached, wondering if his look would give Bailey's fate away. It didn't. He sat down next to me and said, "Bailey's going to make it! None of his arteries or organs were punctured, although he's in pretty bad shape. We stitched and bandaged him up and would like to keep him here for a couple days for observation. He's still in shock and in a lot of pain, as you might imagine."

I felt so relieved and blessed that Bailey survived this terrible ordeal. Recovery was going to be long and slow, but far better than the alternative. I thanked the doctor for all his help and left the animal hospital with deep gratitude.

Deciding to Live

Bailey was not doing well in the hospital, causing great concern among the doctors and nurses. He would not eat or drink and was in a lot of agony. He ended up staying an additional night before the doctors cautiously released him to me, arming me with assorted pills and pain medications.

Once home, I knew the familiar surroundings would provide some comfort for Bailey as he began the recovery process. What I didn't know was how he would respond to being in the backyard again, not to mention seeing the neighbor's two dogs through the newly repaired fence.

Bailey's pain got worse before it got better, leading to some trying moments. Initially, he would snap at me when I would touch him, and he refused to cooperate when I tried to squirt the liquid pain medication into his mouth. As evening came the first night, Bailey was in too much pain to lie down. Eventually, he went out into the back yard with freezing temperatures, and sat by the big tree, not moving. Bailey doesn't like to be cold, and I kept waiting and waiting for him to come inside. I could not understand why he was out there, or why he refused to come in. I tried everything short of grabbing him to coax him inside, but nothing worked.

It was about midnight and I was fighting to stay awake. I feared that the reason Bailey went outside was to die outdoors, and that I'd find his frozen body in my yard in the morning. It was more than I could handle, and I broke down again.

I dozed off. Next thing I knew, it was 5:00 a.m. I shot out of bed, calling Bailey's name. No response. I braced myself as I headed downstairs. I carefully surveyed each room on my way to the sliding glass doors that led to the backyard. No sign of him anywhere. My heart grew heavier and heavier. I opened the sliding glass door and gazed out at the tree where Bailey had been most of the night, afraid of what I might see. But no Bailey there either. Just then the doggy door pushed open and in walked Bailey. His body was cold—but he was alive! He made it through the night.

After those challenging couple of days, Bailey began to improve. Shortly thereafter, a retired couple on my street offered to take care of him during the day until he got better. That was such a blessing.

Probably the biggest change after the attack occurred with me. Although I loved my house of 27 years, my neighbors, and my community, I felt violated. My emotional attachment to my home was gone. I felt nothing.

That was the bad news. The good news was that I sold my house and moved to Wash Park, the neighborhood where I'd always wanted to live.

Amazing how there's a silver lining in even the darkest moments of my life.

P.S. Two years after the attack, Bailey passed away at the age of 15. He lived an amazing life and was surrounded by loved ones when he transitioned. I still think of him every day.

34
What the Game of Golf Taught Me About Life

Seek progress, not perfection.
The perfect swing doesn't exist.

— Leonard Finkel

I'm what's commonly referred to as a "hacker" when it comes to golf. In fact, if you look up hacker in the dictionary it says, "See Greg Giesen." I'm serious. A hacker is someone who never puts the time or effort into improving their golf game; hence it's erratic at best, and never improves.

I want to improve; it's just that I can't seem to recall all of the stuff that I'm supposed to remember when I'm swinging at the ball. It's hard enough being me, with all the voices I already have in my head, let alone all the uninvited golf pros that join the cacophony the moment I step onto the course. It gets a little crowded up there, if you know what I mean.

I've tried to quit the game altogether on numerous occasions. The problem is the golf gods like to play practical jokes on me, especially on the last hole. For whatever reason, my best shot of the day always occurs on the last hole, making me believe that I'm actually improving. How crazy is that?

A few years ago, after quitting golf for the 567,321st time, I had a revelation. Actually, it could have been indigestion, but it led to an insight just the same. It went something like this: *Perhaps the reason I'm terrible at golf is because I'm not applying myself. Maybe I need a more concentrated approach—like intense lessons for four straight days—at a luxury resort in Phoenix—with friends?*

It was as if the golf experts in my head threw me a Hail Mary pass, attempting to salvage what little was left of my game. Perhaps with the right teachers, instruction, equipment, and technique, they reasoned, I could actually improve my game.

Are you buying this so far? I did. And I proceeded to talk some friends and family members into joining me. *Why not!* I figured. *Even if my golf goes south, at least I'll have some fun.*

And Then Reality Set In . . .

I went to the golf school in Phoenix and immersed myself in every little nuance around the game. I developed a new swing. I purchased new clubs. I practiced day and night. I even bought a fancy glove that matched my golf bag. And I studied too. I diligently created a stack of "how-to" tips and put them on index cards so that I could pull them out at any time on the course for direction. I was a golf machine. I looked good, I felt good, and I was confident.

And yet my game got worse.

By the end of the four days, my ball had hit more houses and landed in more pools than a hailstorm. I think the homeowner's association may have issued a warrant for my arrest before I left.

"I quit!" I told my uncle Roger as we drove to the Phoenix airport.

"You can't quit!" he shouted. "You just spend over a thousand dollars on these lessons. You need to give it time."

"I quit," I said. "I don't want to ever see a golf ball as long as I live. I'm done. And I mean it this time," I cried.

He could only shake his head.

The Phoenix Airport

My delayed flight back to Denver gave me an unexpected couple of hours to roam around the airport and check out the various stores and shops. I'm normally not a shopper, but there was a lot of commotion in the little bookstore right across from my gate. I went to see.

As I approached, I noticed that a crowd had gathered around a particular book display.

Ah, I sighed, *that's exactly the distraction I need to get my mind out of this golf funk that I'm in: a nice novel to read on the plane!*

I maneuvered my way over to the display. *What book could possibly be so popular?*

And then the title came into view. *No way! Are you kidding me!*

Sure enough, the one subject I no longer wanted to read about—the one symbol I never wanted to see again—was right there staring me in the face. The cover depicted a golf ball flying over the fairway, as giddy and happy as a golf ball could be. The book was *The Legend of Bagger Vance,* by Steven Pressfield.

I quit, I cried. *Remember!*

As I started to look away, the six-word subtitle caught my attention: *Golf and the Game of Life.*

I quickly looked around to make sure none of my golf school buddies were watching, and I grabbed the book. I was surprised by how comfortable it felt in my hands. And it had that new book smell too. Even the cover was enticing, so I opened it up to a random page.

Call it coincidence or the Universe's way of communicating to me, but what I read challenged my view of life. And it also challenged my perspective on golf.

For those of you not familiar with the story, Bagger Vance is a caddy who mysteriously comes into the life of a struggling golfer and ends up helping him not only turn his game around—but also his life. Here's the excerpt that I read that day in the Phoenix airport, with Bagger Vance narrating:

"I believe that each of us possesses, inside ourselves, one true Authentic Swing that is ours alone. It is folly to try to teach us another, or mold us to some ideal version of the perfect swing. Each player possesses only that one swing that he was born with, that swing which existed within him before he ever picked up a club. Our task as golfers is simply to chip away all that is inauthentic, allowing our Authentic Swing to emerge in its purity."

I felt as though the golf ball on the cover hit me in the head! I was dazed by the powerful message and its many implications.

I've been going at it all wrong! I realized. *Instead of changing my swing, I need to find it. I need to go all the way back before my first golf lesson and embrace my natural swing—the swing I started with—instead of trying to imitate all the many versions that have been imposed on me over the years.*

It suddenly was clear; I had been looking for answers in all the wrong places. I was defining myself—and my swing—by external measures instead of trusting my own internal instincts and desires. And what's worse, I had lost myself in the process.

I smiled. *And to think, all of this from a few sentences in a book!*

But it's true. I had somehow lost my Authentic Swing and maybe even my Authentic Self, by allowing others to define who I was and who I needed to be. You might say I was experiencing an identity crisis on multiple levels.

In the end, I came to realize that releasing all the opinions, standards, and judgments of others, including my own, led me to a much more simplified perspective on life. And it led to a more natural golf swing.

So I tossed out the "how-to" cards, went back to my old clubs, and I stopped keeping score when I played. And guess what? It worked. I started having fun again. That childlike exhilaration that drew me to golf in the first place reappeared. I began noticing the little things like the squishiness of the grass under my shoes as I walked down the fairway; the ping of a club hitting the ball perfectly off the tee, and the sound of the battery-powered beer cart driving up in just the nick of time. You get the idea.

But has my golf game improved, you ask?

Not at all. But it doesn't matter anymore, I'm having fun again.

Bonus

Eight Simple Rules to Managing Conflict

Be kind, for everyone you meet is fighting a hard battle.

— Plato

Managing conflict with coworkers doesn't have to be difficult. Below is a summary of the eight simple rules that I created to help people deal with conflict and improve relationships at work. Each rule also is explained in detail.

Rule 1: Begin with the end in mind

The way we approach a conflict will greatly impact the outcome. The more we focus on a specific goal or outcome, the better able we'll be to stay true to our task.

Rule 2: Stay off the ladder

In any conflict, it is to our advantage, and to the benefit of the relationship in question, that we seek out the facts, information, and perspectives from all parties involved before forming any opinions or taking any action.

Rule 3: Choose your style

Our autopilot response to conflict may not always be the best approach in every situation or with every relationship. We need to think about the other person in the conflict and select an approach (or style) that can best create win-win outcomes.

Rule 4: Take the initiative

The truth is, if a conflict bothers us, then it is ours to resolve. Waiting for the other party to come to us first doesn't help us address the problem; it only prolongs it.

Rule 5: Focus "out" before focusing "in"

Focusing "out" means listening to the other party's point of view before expressing our own. Why does this matter? Because it puts the other person at ease knowing that their concerns have been heard and validated. When people feel listened to and acknowledged, they typically relax and lower their defenses. This not only helps ease the conversation, but also increases the likelihood that the other party will be more willing to hear our side of the story.

Rule 6: Ask for what you need

There is more to conflict than what's on the surface. In most cases, there is an underlying need that is not being met or recognized. In order to fully resolve a conflict, we need to first identify the need that's not being met, and then negotiate from there.

Rule 7: Manage the *How* and the *What* will take care of itself

Successfully managing conflict means having the ability not only to identify an issue, but also to resolve it in a respectful, collaborative manner with the other party. With just a little preparation, we can ease the whole experience and set ourselves and the other party up for success.

Rule 8: Empower the third side

In a conflict, there's *your side*, there's *their side*, and there's the *third side*. According to William Ury, author of *Getting to Peace*, the third side is the impact that a conflict between two team members has on other members of the team. Although many *third siders* see themselves as innocent bystanders, they actually have a tremendous influence on establishing a work environment that either supports constructive conflict resolution or reinforces dysfunctional conflict resolution.

* To watch video discussions of each of the Eight Simple Rules to Managing Conflict, go to www.leadingfromwithin.net.

Rule 1:
Begin with the End in Mind

Mediator: Before we begin today's mediation, I'd like to ask each of you to share what your desired outcome is for today's meeting. Bob, why don't you go first.

Bob: Okay. I guess I'd like to walk out of here with a better understanding of how to communicate better with Jerry.

Mediator: Bob, can you be more specific.

Bob: Sure. Jerry and I have been butting heads a lot lately and I don't know what I'm doing that's triggering him so much.

Mediator: So, you want to know if you are bothering Jerry when you talk to him and, if so, how to make that different.

Bob: Yes.

Mediator: And Jerry, what's your desired outcome?

Jerry: Frankly, I just want Bob to leave me alone. Just let me do my job.

Mediator: Jerry, is it the way Bob approaches you or the frequency that's the issue for you?

Jerry: The frequency. Bob is an okay guy.

Mediator: So, you'd like Bob to be more respectful of your time.

Jerry: Yes.

And the mediation goes on . . .

What the dialogue above demonstrates is Rule 1: Begin with the End in Mind.

Over my 20+ years as a conflict mediator, I have found that we are more effective in conflict when we are prepared, focused on a desired goal or outcome, and have a plan. When we are prepared and focused on what we want, we are less distracted by the things that may divert us from a successful resolution, such as personality differences, temperament, tension, and past history with a particular individual. Being goal-focused also helps us remain calm, cool, and collected when addressing conflict because there is an intentionality to our communication. This is how we need to be in conflicting situations.

When I mediate a conflict between two people, I begin with a separate coaching session with each party. The purpose of this added step is three-fold. First, I help both parties identify a desired outcome and a win-win strategy for the mediation session. Second, I establish a level of trust between the parties and myself. Since part of my job is to create a safe space for the mediation, it is essential that I'm trusted as a mediator, facilitator, and coach. Third, by taking time to prepare for the mediation, both parties are ready to talk and reach resolution the moment they walk into the room. That's because they are focused on outcomes.

I want to mention here that I'm not advocating for a third-party mediator, like myself, to help resolve a conflict. I believe there is a time and place when a third-party should be considered, but only as a last resort. What I am advocating for is taking the time to focus on desired outcomes before engaging in a conflicting dynamic with another person. Lead with the head and not the heart.

But what about those "in-the-moment" conflicts that don't allow for any kind of preparation?

Have a Plan B—an escape route. As mentioned, we don't do conflict well when we aren't prepared. What's the point of getting caught up in a conflict or interpersonal argument when all we are going to do is get mad, defensive, emotional, and ultimately damage the relationship? My advice—don't engage! If it's a stranger—avoid, leave, or let it go. If it is a colleague, friend, or family member—postpone the discussion. You can decide later on how to proceed or even if you need to.

There is one more influencing factor to consider when we talk about Rule 1: Begin with the End in Mind.

Let me ask you this:

When you think about the word conflict, does it bring up more negative or positive connotations and why?

When you reflect on your own past conflicts, would you say that you generally handled them effectively, ineffectively, or not at all?

This is important because our past experiences with conflict have formed our autopilot response, which is hard to alter. As a result, if our overriding perception of conflict is negative, we'll be more likely to avoid it, deny it, mismanage it, sit on it, resist it, or project it onto the other person. And we'll do this without much thought. This is because we associate conflict as a threat and automatically go into self-protective mode—which is unlikely to be effective.

Conversely, if we've had primarily good experiences with past conflicts, we'll be more inclined to resolve, encourage, address, move past, and/or bring new issues out in the open. That's because we've already formed a positive association with conflict resolution.

Why is this important?

Because in situations where we have a predisposition to view conflict as negative, our ability to focus on outcomes (Rule 1) is even more important. It means overriding our autopilot response with a conscious focus on outcomes.

Case in point: My autopilot response to conflict is to internalize it. I have a tendency to go inside my head where I proceed to analyze the problem at great lengths. Sometimes I find a resolution and sometimes I end up doing nothing. Either way, I don't always involve the other party in this process. Sometimes they don't even know there is an issue. Can you see how that could be problematic?

In my case, internalizing conflict won't help me if I value and want to maintain a relationship with the person I'm in conflict with. Hence, I need to be mindful of my tendency and always communicate with the other party so that resolution is a collaborative process.

In conclusion, *Begin with the End in Mind* means:

- Prepare ahead of time

- Identify a desired outcome prior to engagement

- Seek win-win resolutions where both parties benefit

- Visualize a positive conversation and setting a positive intent

- Override all auto-responses that don't serve us in the moment

- Walk away from "in-the-moment" conflicts if we're either not prepared or too emotionally charged. If these involve a relationship that matters to us, then we can revisit the conversation when we've had time to prepare.

Rule 2:
Stay Off the Ladder

Have you ever been cut off by a driver on the highway and then instantly given them "feedback?"

Have you ever said something to someone that you didn't mean?

Have you ever judged someone only to find out later that you were wrong?

If you answered "yes" to any of the above questions, congratulations! You may not know it, but you have already climbed *the* "Ladder of Inference."

Rule 2: Stay off the Ladder, refers to the Ladder of Inference from Peter Senge's book, *The Fifth Discipline*, where Senge uses the ladder as a metaphor to talk about how we create beliefs based on false assumptions. Allow me to explain using my *tweaked* version of Senge's model (created with permission).

Let's take the example of giving some instant feedback to the person who just cut you off on the highway. Here's essentially what you did, starting from the bottom of the ladder and moving up—and all in a matter of seconds:

1. While driving, you are cut off by another driver. *First rung.*
2. You are able to avoid a collision but are fuming at the other driver. It's all you can think about. *Second rung.*
3. You immediately assess that the other driver was not paying attention. *Third rung.*
4. You decide that anyone who doesn't pay attention while driving is an idiot. *Fourth rung.*
5. You also notice the driver has out-of-town plates from Nebraska and it fits in with your stereotype of Nebraska drivers. *Fifth rung.*
6. You decide that Nebraska drivers are dangerous, and you need to avoid them. You speed past the driver to get away. *Sixth rung.*
7. While passing, you flash a gesture at the driver. *Seventh rung.*

In the above example, you went from the bottom of the ladder to the top in just a few seconds. That doesn't mean each of us methodically goes from rung to rung, but we do take an incident, make assumptions and judgments around it, and very often take an action as a result.

The problem with racing up the ladder toward action is:

- The more emotion we have, the faster we climb the ladder. The faster we climb, the less control we have over the outcome. The less control we have over the outcome, the more accelerated the conflict can get.

- We do not live in a *stimulus* → *response* world. Nobody makes us feel a certain way. Nobody causes us to respond in a particular manner. Nobody is responsible for our actions but us. When we immediately respond to a stimulus (i.e., being cut off), we have removed the thought process from the situation and allowed our emotions to take over. This leads to a *stimulus* → *response* mind-set where we get to blame somebody or something for our response. Not good.

In truth, there's actually a three-step process that takes place, not two: There is an activating event (Step 1); there is our assessment of the activating event (Step 2); and there is our response to the activating event (Step 3). In other words, Step 1 did not cause Step 3; Step 2 caused Step 3; and Step 2 is about us, not about them!

The good news here is that when we are mindful of our reactions, we can stop climbing the ladder before acting. We can regain control in the moment and choose to respond from a logical place. Or to put it another way, we can begin the process of climbing down the ladder.

There is also an important missing piece when we go up the ladder. Do you know what it is?

It's the other side of the story. It's understanding *why* someone did what they did. It's getting *all* the information before choosing a response.

You see, the Ladder of Inference is a one-sided process. It allows us to play judge and jury over someone else's actions and make a conviction without ever hearing the other side. The so-called upside is that we get to be right. But the reality is that it's not a fair process. It's not fair to the other party nor is it fair to us.

IT'S ALL ABOUT ME!

The key here is to: *observe*

- Turn a primarily unconscious process into a conscious process, (i.e., noticing when we are going up the ladder.)

- Not respond to an activating event until we have all the facts.

- Catch ourselves going up the ladder and coach ourselves back down.

- Slow down all *stimulus* ⟶ *response* behavior patterns where we surrender control over how we respond. By simply not responding automatically, we introduce thought into the process.

- Always give the benefit of doubt in situations or with people where we do not have all the information on what's going on. After all, wouldn't you want someone else to give you the same respect?

A buddy of mine who also uses the Ladder of Inference model came up to me one day and said, "You mentioned something yesterday that concerned me, and I found myself going up the ladder. Instead of doing that, I wanted to just come out and ask you directly to better understand what you meant."

When I heard my buddy say that to me, I respected him even more than I already did. He not only took responsibility for his interpretation of what I said, but he also came to me for clarification.

I have found through my mediation work that misperceptions are the culprit that start many conflicts—misperceptions that turn into assumptions, conclusions, beliefs, and actions. This why we need to be mindful of our own ladders and make sure we have all the information before taking an action.

Lastly, there's the Bypass on the Ladder of Inference. The bypass essentially means that our beliefs about someone or something are so strong that any new data to the contrary will be disregarded in order to preserve our certainty.

Here's an example why the bypass is so dangerous:

A couple that my ex-wife and I used to invite over for dinner would cancel at the last minute on a fairly frequent basis. In fact, it happened so regularly that we had a "bypass" going on about their ability to keep a commitment. Sure enough, the night before we were once again supposed to get together, I received a call and could see it was from them. Before answering, I gave my wife a familiar glance and proceeded to shake my head in disappointment as I answered, already knowing they were cancelling yet again.

"Hello."

"Greg, this is Ray."

"Ray, how nice to hear from you," I said sarcastically.

"Bad news . . . we are not going to be able to make it over tomorrow."

Looking over at my wife, I point to the phone to indicate that I was right.

"Oh, that's terrible. Is everything okay?" I asked, not really interested in hearing another excuse.

"Jenny's parents are coming into town tomorrow."

And you schedule this knowing we were supposed to get together, I thought. "Okay, maybe next time," I said, knowing that there probably wouldn't be a next time.

A couple of days later, I found out the rest of the story. Jen had been diagnosed with stage 4 cancer. Her parents were coming into town to be with her.

I felt terrible. I was so certain that I was right (the bypass) about our friends that I didn't leave any room for other options.

The bypass prevents relationships or situations from improving. It's unhealthy, damaging, and usually unfair.

If you have a bypass with a person that matters to you, talk it out and work through it. Otherwise, your relationship will be stuck and won't get better. Why would you want a relationship like that?

Likewise, if people have formed a bypass about us, we can only hope they will talk it out with us instead of holding it against us. They need to hear our perspective as well.

So, that's Rule 2 in a nutshell. Stay off the ladder!

Rule 3:
Choose Your Style

(A conversation during a recent coaching session)

Me: Tom, how are things going with Nancy?

Tom: Well . . . not that great actually.

Me: What do you mean? Last time we talked you were all excited about dating her.

Tom: I know, but things have changed. She's blown me off.

Me: Wait, weren't you just with her a week ago? What happened?

Tom: She just stopped communicating. She was supposed to call me on Monday and never called. On Tuesday, she was going over to a mutual friend of ours, and we were going to get together later that night, and she blew me off then as well. No call, no text, no email. Zero! Nada!

Me: So, what did you do?

Tom: Since we had planned to go out to a fancy restaurant for New Year's, I texted her in the morning and asked if we were still going. And guess what? No response yet again. Can you believe it? So, I cancelled our reservations and broke the news to her in a text.

Me: Why didn't you just call her?

Tom: I had already called earlier in the week with no luck. What do you think I'm a glutton for punishment?

Me: Okay, I'm assuming she didn't respond to your latest text either.

Tom: Correct; that is until today. And get this, she said she had an unexpected out-of-town guest show up and hadn't looked at her cell phone for the past three days. She said she was sorry we missed our dinner.

Me: How did that make you feel?

Tom: Like I'm an idiot! Come on Geese, I wasn't born yesterday. Does she sound like someone who is interested in developing a relationship with me? Didn't check her cell phone for three days! Seriously! This is a woman who is attached to her phone. She lives on her Facebook app.

Me: So, is it over?

Tom: It is for me.

Me: Are you going to tell her?

Tom: Why should I? She's the one who stopped communicating with me. What would be the point?

Me: What do you gain by not communicating?

Tom: She gets some of her own medicine. Let's see how she likes it!

Me: So, is the noncommunication a form of retaliation?

Tom: You just don't treat people that way.

Me: Who are you talking about Tom, you or her?

Tom: She started it. She disrespected me first. That's not right.

Me: I only bring it up because it seemed like you really cared for her.

Tom: Never again. Burn me once, shame on you, burn me twice, shame on me.

Me: Is not communicating a trigger for you?

Tom: Yes. My mother would stop talking to me when she was upset. It drove me crazy.

Me: What did you do then?

Tom: I shut down too. We'd play this game of not talking to each other. It sometimes went on for days.

Me: How would it usually end with your mother?

Tom: Eventually one of us would slowly start talking to the other. In most cases she'd be the one to break the silence.

Me: Why not you?

Tom: Because I was mad at her for shutting down communication, so I refused to give in. I guess I was punishing her in a way.

Me: Sounds similar to what you are doing with Nancy.

Tom: I guess so.

Me: Would it be fair to say that you're an "avoider" when it comes to conflict?

Tom: Not always. But it's probably what I do when I'm really upset with someone.

Me: But when you do that, doesn't it actually prolong the conflict? You've already mentioned that shutting down communication is a trigger for you. In essence, it prevents the conflict from being resolved.

Tom: (Being funny) Yeah, so what's your point?

Me: Would you say that the pattern of shutting down or avoiding communication around a conflicting issue has caused more harm than good for you?

Tom: Probably.

Me: Probably?

Tom: Okay, yes it has, Dr. Phil.

Me: I'm just trying to help here. What other options exist in these situations?

Tom: I guess I could assert myself instead of always reacting and responding to the other person.

Me: Ah, that would be a different approach. By shutting down, you end up giving them all the power in the relationship. Can you see that?

Tom: I can now.

Me: But by being assertive and talking about the issue, you take back the power and you get to end the conflict, instead of dragging it out.

Tom: Point made. Maybe it comes down to self-respect. I need to respect myself first.

Me: Exactly. By standing up for yourself, you are truly respecting yourself. You're also changing the pattern that you've followed for years, and thereby changing the dynamic of your relationships. All of that can happen when you choose to respond differently when triggered.

Tom: But what if it doesn't work?

Me: If you stay consistent around it, people will eventually accept the new you. If you are erratic and only sometimes assert yourself, you'll be sending mixed messages and then it could very well backfire. Consistency is the key.

Tom: You want me to call Nancy, don't you?

Me: Why wait to change the pattern, when you can do it now?

The above true story introduces the concept of Rule 3: Choose Your Style. When I explain this concept in the classroom, I introduce the five different Thomas Kilmann Conflict Styles—Avoiding, Accommodating, Compromising, Collaborating, and Forcing—and have the participants identify which style best describes their "go-to" behavior under most circumstances.

My intent in this exercise is to emphasize the importance of *choosing* the most appropriate style for the conflict at hand, as opposed to embodying any one style. What do I mean? The key to any conflict resolution process is to separate ourselves from the conflict. When we are overly attached to the conflict, as Tom was in the preceding scenario, our egos, hurt feelings, and self-protectiveness quickly take over and embed us more deeply in the conflict. Tom's relationship with Nancy didn't have to end, but Tom got so caught up in the dynamics that he lost sight of the options that were available to him. As a result, he didn't choose a conflict style but instead slipped into his "go-to" style or "default" style of avoidance. Granted, avoidance may have been the most comfortable style for him but clearly it was not the most effective. Tom had an opportunity to change an ineffective pattern from his past, but instead, he reinforced it. He acted based on emotion and hurt feelings, not on logic.

A colleague of mine said it best: We have a bow and a quiver with five arrows at our disposal at any given time. Each arrow represents one of the five conflict styles. When in a conflict, we need to keep our eye on the bull's-eye (the desired outcome) and choose the arrow that will get us there most accurately.

Designed by Wannapik
www.wannapik.com

IT'S ALL ABOUT ME!

If we don't choose an arrow, then our default arrow becomes our arrow of choice. The problem is that our default arrow has more to do with familiarity and self-protection than conflict resolution. More often, it's not the best choice.

Among the five conflict styles, there are appropriate and inappropriate uses for each one. For example, avoiding can be an effective response to conflict when we have a run-in with a stranger. Why? Because it's not someone we have an invested relationship with, and it might be dangerous to escalate. However, avoiding communication with a person we care for leaves an unresolved issue floating over the relationship. This is why it is so important to step back from the conflict and choose a style that will lead to a desired outcome.

If you are not familiar with the Thomas Kilmann Conflict Styles, go to http://www.kilmanndiagnostics.com/ to learn more. Also, there are many YouTube videos on the model.

Rule 4:
Take the Initiative

. . . In the event of a loss of cabin pressure, an oxygen mask will drop from above. Tighten the mask by pulling on the straps like this. If you are traveling with a child, place your mask on first before assisting them. . .

Whenever I hear that part of the flight attendant's preflight spiel, I always smile. I smile because my gut instinct would be to place the mask on a child first. But I get it: save yourself so you can save others!

The same principle applies to Rule 4: Take the Initiative. Too often, we lose ourselves in the dynamics of a conflict. We may take on much more of the burden than we should. This happens when we become frustrated or angry and we cut off communication, or we retaliate, or we refuse to hear the other party's perspective, or we refuse to forgive until we get a proper apology.

In each of the actions above, we are essentially empowering the other person by reacting and responding, instead of focusing on ourselves and what we need. In essence, we are putting the proverbial oxygen mask on them first before ourselves. See the difference?

Who, but our ego, really cares about who started the conflict or who should apologize first or who's right and who's wrong? When we lose our focus, we can become caught up in insignificant nuances which, more often than not, lead to a stalemate.

Let me give you an example. A couple of months ago I was introduced to an insurance broker who agreed to help me obtain a new health insurance plan. He was a nice guy and initially very helpful, until I was rejected by the insurance company. Suddenly our relationship seemed to change as he stopped using the "we" pronoun and suggested "I" appeal the decision on my own. Then he stopped communicating with me. No help, no advice, no plan B, nothing. It felt like I was left for roadkill.

Now as I saw it, I had two options. I could either be angry, hold a grudge, and retaliate by seeking out a new broker, or I could initiate contact with my current broker and focus on what I need (i.e., guidance, advice, and a commitment to help me), especially now.

Initially, I wanted to give him a piece of my mind about his client-relationship skills, but how was that going to help me get my needs met? If anything, it would create more unwanted tension, strife and distraction, which was the last thing I needed. So, I let go of being a victim, being right, and being hurt. Instead, I called him, and we were able to get back on the same page with no lasting damage to the relationship.

When we take the initiative to resolve a conflict:

- We get our own needs met.

- We hold the other party accountable by bringing the conversation to them.

- We release the burden of holding grudges, stress, or pent-up emotions.

- We stay off the ladder.

- We role model effective conflict resolution.

- We effectively manage the relationship.

When we don't take the initiative, the opposite will likely be true. Our needs won't be met, there will be no accountability with the other party, and anger and frustration will fester. In this way, we role model ineffective conflict resolution, and we enable a dysfunctional relationship.

Not good.

The solution is to know what you want (Rule 1), let go of judgments and assumptions that can get in the way (Rule 2), choose an approach that will get you to resolution (Rule 3), and initiate a conversation (Rule 4) so you get what you need. In so doing, you will dramatically increase your likelihood of resolving any conflict.

Rule 5:
Focus *Out* Before Focusing *In*

"I need a volunteer . . . Greg?"

Wow, that felt more like telling than asking, I thought. "Sure Ron, I'd be glad to volunteer."

Ron asked me to stand in front of the group as he approached. I knew he picked me for a reason but wasn't quite sure why. And then he hit my chest with such force that I stumbled back a couple of steps.

"What are you doing?" I yelled, trying to regain my composure.

"What do you think?" he said, as he wound up for a second attack.

My classmates were in shock. Their eyes glued on Ron, trying to determine if they should watch the frontal assault or intervene.

I braced myself.

WHAM! With both hands he struck my chest again. "What did you say?" he screamed.

Clearly Ron was trying to unravel me. I was determined not to engage. I smiled, "I didn't say anything, Ron."

He lunged at me again and then again. Each time I took a step back and absorbed the blow. I pictured being Gumby and relaxed my body with each punch. He got angrier and angrier.

Photo from www.pinterest

"Stop it!" yelled Mary, one of my classmates.

The tension in the room was intense—for everyone but me. Ron continued to attack, and I continued to step back and absorb. Finally, out of exhaustion, he stopped and shook his head.

"You asshole," and gave up.

The Lesson

That confrontation was Ron's way of teaching by example. He was my graduate school professor and we were talking about conflict in class. He picked me as his subject because I had not yet shown any vulnerability in class and he wanted to demonstrate how easily he could draw me into an emotional confrontation. Only it didn't work.

Had I not been on display in front of my classmates, I probably would have gotten upset with Ron and overtly resisted his attack. But because I was so aware that I was "on stage," I maintained self-control by focusing on him rather than myself. This helped me better anticipate, absorb, and diffuse what was coming next. It is also the premise behind Rule 5: Focus Out Before Focusing In.

Focusing Out Before Focusing In means understanding the problem completely from the other person's side before trying to assert our own. Or, as the late, great Stephen Covey would say, "Seek first to understand, then to be understood." And, the best way to focus out is through listening. That's right. I'm talking about the ability to listen from a place of curiosity, sincerity, and openness, with a focus to truly understand.

From my experience, the easiest way to diffuse an angry person is by showing them that we care about them and about their concerns equally. We do this by respectfully listening and asking questions to ensure that we fully understand what's going on for them. When people feel heard, when people feel validated, when people feel cared for, their anger dissipates, and their defenses soften. More importantly, they begin to feel connected to us and are more willing to reciprocate by understanding our perspective.

It's both that simple and that difficult.

I was speaking at a workshop when a woman in the audience took offense to something I said. She angrily rose from her seat and began to verbally attack me. Shocked, I could tell that this was more of a misunderstanding than anything else. However, instead of interrupting her, arguing with her, or telling her she misunderstood, I took the time to listen and paraphrase back to her what I heard her saying. She looked up at me, somewhat surprised, and said, "Yes, that's it." I then apologized for my delivery and explained what I had meant to say. She smiled and thanked me for clarifying.

Can you see how this was no different than how I responded to Ron, when he pushed me around the room? Instead of protecting myself through defending or resisting a verbal or physical attack, I focused out. I listened to her words and calmly paraphrased them back to show understanding. I diffused the verbal assault, as I had done with Ron.

John Heider, author of *The Tao of Leadership*, once told me to imagine seeing the words *TEACH ME* above the head of every person that I have any conflict with as a way of reminding me to focus out before focusing in.

> *Teach me* what's upsetting you and why.
> *Teach me* how I may have contributed to the problem
> and what I can do to fix it.
> *Teach me* how to work with you so that we can
> collaborate better.
> *Teach me* . . . *Teach me* . . . *Teach me* . . .

And it worked!

Rule 6:
Ask for What You Need

I had a love-hate relationship with my former boss, Terry McDougal. I had incredible respect for this former Olympic gold medalist turned CEO of one of the leading professional development companies in the world. He could make an audience laugh, cry, and feel inspired—all at the same time. People always came up to me after one of Terry's amazing speeches to say how lucky I was to work for this man. I'd smile and say, "I sure am." But I was lying through my teeth.

In hindsight, it was awfully ironic. We were a company best known for our leadership development programs and materials, and yet we didn't practice what we preached. We were a walking contradiction.

Terry ran the organization with an iron fist. Command and control. It was a classic parent-child dynamic between Terry and his managers. And I was the newest. He was a short man who sat behind a desk so large that he literally looked down at whoever sat in one of the two little chairs across from him.

Whenever Terry wanted to see you, he wanted to see you NOW. Not in ten minutes, not when you have time, but NOW! And since he was a man of few words, he'd never tell you why. As a result, you didn't know if you were in trouble or if you would be expected to summarize something from a past report that he's finally read. All you got was, "Can you come down to my office!" It wasn't a question, but rather a demand—and it was agonizing for me.

Terry's office was on the opposite side of the building, in its own wing. The laborious walk required traversing an unending maze of long hallways, until you'd eventually pop out right in front of his old and grouchy secretary, who never seemed to know you were coming.

"What do you want?" she'd say, without looking up. It was awful.

The part that baffles me to this day, is how all the other managers seemed okay with Terry's abrupt and controlling style. In fact, they almost welcomed the dysfunction, enabling it whenever possible. In hindsight, I think Terry's ineptness provided comic relief for them. And get this: every Friday, all the managers would sneak out to lunch (we didn't want Terry to know we were getting together) and meet up at a local restaurant where we'd take turns sharing Terry stories over beers (keep in mind this was more than 20 years ago).

But for me, the Terry bashing didn't alleviate or justify his behavior. I still struggled with it and one Friday decided to bring it up at lunch. "I just don't think it is right," I said, "And he needs to know that we can't always come running every time he needs something."

The other managers laughed. "Are you serious? The last guy to take on Terry was immediately shown the door." And they all nodded.

So much for their support, I realized.

As the weeks went by, my resolve to change my relationship with Terry increased with every interaction. I thought and thought and thought. I knew that his sense of urgency and abruptness was annoying, but there had to be something else. Why was he making me so mad?

And then it came to me!

It wasn't the immediacy factor and it wasn't his bark—it was not knowing what he wanted that was killing me. Terry never took the time to set a context for his requests. He waited until you were standing in front of him before explaining himself. I felt incompetent every time I walked into his office. Plus, it wasn't an efficient use of time, and I'd usually have to run back and forth to my office to get information or a file that I hadn't known to bring.

I hated the power game. Because I didn't know what Terry wanted, I was helpless, vulnerable, and unprepared. This was not a desirable place for me. I'm the type of guy who will go to great lengths to be prepared for just about anything I do.

I've Identified the Root of the Problem, Now What?

This is where *Rule 6*: Ask for What You Need comes in. I wanted Terry to tweak his behavior just enough so I could feel more competent and so we could have more efficient meetings. And all he would have to do is take an extra few seconds to explain why he needed to see me before hanging up the phone. That's not asking too much, is it?

The key to asking for what you need with your boss is to make it a mutually beneficial request, thereby giving your boss incentive to change. Some call this "managing up"—and they are correct. It's the same thing.

But isn't this a form of manipulation, you ask?

Yes and no. *Yes*—in that you are purposely crafting your words to solicit a desired response, but *No*—in that you are simply asking for what you need. What we are talking about here is diplomacy. Instead of criticizing your boss, you can turn your unmet need into a request. The end results are the same—your boss changes his/her behavior and your needs are met. And you don't have to upset your boss in the process. How cool is that?

So, Here's How It Went Down

At the end of our weekly one-on-one meeting I said, "Terry, there's one more thing."

"What's that?" he said.

"You know what would be helpful to me?"

"What's that?" he said again.

"When you need me ASAP, do you mind taking a second or two to tell me what it's about? That way I can be more prepared and not have to waste your time by running back and forth to my office."

He smiled, "Sure."

I did a double take. *Sure! That's it! You mean to tell me I've spent all these months agonizing over this and that's all you have to say?*

But it worked! By phrasing what I needed in a win-win request, how could he say no. It also made it easy to gently remind Terry of our agreement the few times he forgot later on.

So, the next time you are in a conflict and have needs not being met, your first obligation is to simply ask, in a respectful way, for what you need. In preparation, follow these steps:

1. Identify what you need
2. Determine what that would look like behaviorally
3. Turn it into a request
4. Emphasize the mutual benefits

This is the same process I use when mediating a conflict between two employees. Instead of focusing on the problematic behavior, I have them negotiate around what needs aren't being met. Then they form requests, make agreements, and move on.

Unmet needs are what cause most conflicts. That should be one of the first places to explore if we really want to understand why we are in a conflict in the first place.

Rule 7:
Manage the *How* and the *What* will Take Care of Itself

There are two components to every argument or conflict. There's the conflicting issue (the *what*) and there's the interpersonal dynamics surrounding the conflict (the *how*). Guess which one is most important?

Very simply, how you *do* conflict will directly impact the outcome of the conflict itself. If you are kind, respectful, collaborative, and focused on win-win outcomes, you'll get one result. If you are mean, rude, aggressive, and focused on being right, you'll get an entirely different one.

The *how* sets up the *what*. Failure to effectively manage the *how* means all bets are off as to the success of the resolution. When you focus on the issue without any attention to the interpersonal dynamics, you are asking for a fight; a fight that could do some serious long-term damage to your spouse, partner, colleague, or friend.

Okay, you say, but what if it's just the clerk at the store I'm in conflict with?

No difference. It's still a relationship.

Think about it. How would you want to be treated if someone confronted you? Would you want them to be respectful or hard charging and in your face?

It's not complicated. If you can manage the *how*, then the *what* will take care of itself. Here are some initial suggestions for managing the *how*:

- Begin with the end in mind (Rule 1). Have a plan—know what you want—and move the conversation in that direction.

- Avoid going up the ladder (Rule 2) and making assumptions until you have all the information to work with.

- Use a conflict style (Rule 3) that is best suited for getting win-win results.

- Take the initiative (Rule 4) to talk with the other party, regardless of who you think is in the right, and who you think is in the wrong.

- Focus on understanding the problem from their perspective first, before expressing yours (Rule 5).

- Be prepared to ask for what you need (Rule 6) and to ask the other party for what they need from you.

In the end, it's all about respect! It's about how you feel in the other person's presence during a confrontation, and how they feel in yours. If both of you feel respected, heard, acknowledged, and appreciated in the presence of the other, then the *what* part of the conflict will be easy. The reverse also is true.

As I have mentioned before in this series, the biggest key to effectively resolving conflict is preparation. When we have time to prepare, we do much better in resolving conflict than when all we can do is react.

Below is the two-step process I use that manages both the *how* and the *what*, when successfully mediating and resolving conflict between two people.

Part I: The Preparation Phase

When preparing for mediation, it is critical to conduct a thorough self-assessment. Here are the questions I use to help conflicting parties think through the conflict. These self-reflection questions are also useful for resolving the typical everyday conflicts and disagreements that we all face.

1. Is the conflict about an isolated event that shows little consistency with the rest of the relationship, or is it the latest in a series of conflicts revealing problems within the relationship as a whole?
2. Are my expectations realistic on how I think things need to be resolved?
3. Am I letting my expectations be shaped or distorted by other people not involved in the conflict?
4. Are my expectations taking into account the other party's needs, values, and constraints?
5. What have I done to contribute to the cause and perpetuation of the conflict?
6. What misperceptions might the other party have of me?
7. What misperceptions might I have of the other party?
8. How are my needs different than the other party's?
9. What am I willing to do to show the other party my willingness to work through our issue?
10. What are some of the workable compromises I can come to the table with?

By using these questions to self-assess and prepare, parties in conflict can put their focus more toward obtaining resolution than finding fault. Thinking through these questions also helps remove any of the emotion that prevents moving forward in a logical manner.

Part II: The Conflict Resolution Process (Formal)

I'm calling this a "formal" process because it is to be used when both parties need a structured format, particularly in cases where the working relationship is strained. I also use this process as my outline when mediating conflicts. Keep in mind, it can be applied to suit a variety of situations.

Step 1: The Face-to-Face Meeting

Opening

- Each party states their intentions and desired outcomes for the meeting.
- Each party acknowledges the importance of their working relationship with each other as well as the importance of reaching resolution.

Step 2: Defining Needs

- Party 1 defines his/her concern with Party 2 and the impact it is having.
- Party 2 summarizes what he/she heard.
- Party 1 describes what he/she needs from the other to correct the problem and seeks agreement from Party 2.
- Party 2 defines his/her concern with Party 1 and the impact it is having.
- Party 1 summarizes what he/she heard.
- Party 2 describes what he/she needs from the other to correct the problem and seeks agreement from Party 1.

Step 3: Additional Issues

- Both parties have an opportunity to raise any additional issues/concerns (following the format above).

Step 4: Summary and Wrap-Up

- Once all problems, concerns, and conflicting issues have been discussed and resolved, both parties summarize together what agreements they made.

- Both parties identify an agreed-upon process for resolving any future conflicts or disagreements that arise.
- Both parties commit to a check-in time/date in the future to revisit the agreements and make any needed adjustments.

This format gives you an example of how the flow of the mediation should go. Every step is essential, from the opening comments to setting a future check-in time between parties.

Some Final Thoughts

My role as a conflict mediator is to manage both the *how* and the *what* in a conversation between two people. What I've found over the years is that when both parties are prepared and goal-focused, rarely do I have to coach them around *how* they are communicating with each other or *what* they are communicating about. That's because they enter into the mediation already focused on reaching resolution.

It comes down to this: If you value the relationship with the person you're in conflict with, then it's worth putting in a little extra time in the preparation phase. It will not only benefit the relationship in the long-run, but you'll also be role modeling to others what effective conflict resolution looks like. And isn't that how it should be?

Rule 8: Empower the Third Side

Christian called the group together. "Gather up, everybody. There's one more thing to take care of before dinner."

We all were pretty exhausted after having just hiked for most of the day wearing 60-pound packs. It was the fourth day of a 10-day Outward Bound program in the Colorado mountains, and nobody was in the mood for another one of Christian's team building activities.

"We've got a problem," he began before correcting himself. "Actually, *you* have a problem."

We all looked around at each other, wondering what was coming next.

He continued, "Jonathan and David have been going at each other for the past two days and it's time this gets resolved."

You've got to be kidding me! I thought. *Why don't you just tell the two of them to fix the problem? Why do the rest of us need to be a part of this!*

Christian looked right at me, as if he could read my mind. "Greg, did you have a question?"

"Ah, well . . . no, not exactly," I stammered, before taking a big breath to regain my confidence. "But, I'm a little confused."

"You're wondering why I'm making this a group issue?" he inquired.

Before I could respond, Kelly, one of the nine other participants sitting in our sort of tribal council circle, spoke up. "But isn't this Jonathan and David's responsibility to resolve their differences?"

"If they can, certainly. But, Kelly, when does it become a team issue?" asked Christian.

Both Jonathan and David were clearly uncomfortable being the focus of this conversation. Neither would look at each other, or at the group.

"I guess if they can't resolve it," she said, a bit meekly.

"I'm still unclear why that makes it a team issue?" I countered. "It's an issue between the two of them, not us. Maybe I'm only speaking for myself, but I'm not really impacted by their relationship with each other."

Half the group nodded with me while the other half looked stunned by what I just said. "I'm just being honest," I added.

Christian welcomed the debate. "Let me ask you a question. When you are out in the wilderness together for eight days, how important is it for you to be a team?"

"Extremely," shouted Valerie, another member of the group. "Our lives depend on it."

Everyone nodded.

"Okay, and what would *being* a team look like?"

Jonathan raised his hand, deciding it was time to be a part of the conversation instead of the object of it. "We'd collaborate and problem solve together, support each other, and help each other out."

"And what about trust?" asked Christian.

Everyone answered at the same time before letting David have the floor. "All those things Jonathan mentioned create the trust."

"I like that," said Kelly.

Christian nodded. "So, is it important for a team that needs to collaborate, problem solve, provide support, and trust each other to also handle interpersonal conflicts effectively?"

"Of course!" shouted the group.

"Then why in the hell aren't you doing it?" retaliated Christian. "Jonathan and David have been bickering back and forth for two days now while the rest of you look away, as if it's not your problem. Well I've got news for you, it is your problem. If two of your teammates are struggling, then all of you are struggling. Every one of you is a reflection of this team; and a team divided is not a team! It's time to walk your talk. Let's see the collaboration. Let's see the problem solving. Let's see the support and trust. Show me!"

I was totally blown away. *Of course, he's right,* I thought. *How can we say we are a team when we can't even address the dynamics within our team! We were living a lie and it was time to step up and be the team that we claimed to be.*

The Third Side

Christian showed us that conflict within a team is a team issue, even when the conflict doesn't directly involve every member. It's what William Ury refers to as the "Third Side" of conflict. According to Ury, there's more to conflict than their side and your side; there's the third side! The third side is the experience of all the people who are impacted by the conflict, whether family members, friends, or colleagues.

Conflict rarely is an isolated event between two people or a group of people. As in the Outward Bound example, Jonathan and David's conflict impacted the rest of the team. Specifically:

- It created tension that was felt by everyone

- It created a breakdown in communication between two people, which meant a breakdown in team communication

- It divided the team, as people inevitably took sides

- It revealed that the team values were being inconsistently applied

Until Christian's intervention, eight of us disassociated ourselves from Jonathan and David's conflict. We failed to realize both the impact it was having on us, and the role we played in enabling the conflict to continue.

Ury believes that there is no middle ground for third siders. He calls on them to rise and engage in the conflicts around them so that: 1) the people in the conflict realize the far-reaching impact their conflict is having on others; and 2) those impacted by the conflict, whether directly or indirectly, can hold the conflicting parties responsible and accountable to resolve their differences in a supportive and constructive manner.

We became a team the moment we all helped Jonathan and David resolve their differences. It was the moment we all took responsibility for the dynamics in the group. It also served as a motivator to resolve any future conflicts immediately, so as to avoid a group intervention. A double benefit, if you will.

This is why Empowering the Third Side is Rule 8. It's a call to action to the people impacted by conflict, as well as those in the conflict, to work through disagreement and strife. With a strong third side, true teamwork will become the norm and not an exception.

Acknowledgments

The stories and insights from this book span over 45 years. Needless to say, a lot of people have had a positive and impactful influence on me during that time and deserve recognition.

Dave Berilla played a critical role at Western State College in mentoring and guiding me in both my personal and professional development. I'm eternally grateful to have him in my life.

Larry Beeson and John Horan introduced me to the funeral industry and connected me to the most amazing professionals that I've ever met.

Tim Lane and I created the Leading From Within program back in 1997 and I'm still offering a version of the 3-day workshop. I'd like to recognize all the cofacilitators that have been a part of this transformational program. They include: Mike Kraft, Tom Crouser, Krista Barbour, Larry "Beese" Beeson, Mike Bleier, Shelly Spaulding, Kelly Wyngarden, Steve Sorenson, and Kevin O'Herron.

Christian Itin is one of the most amazing outdoor education facilitators I've ever been around. I'd like to thank him and the Colorado Outward Bound organization for providing the programs that inspired many of the stories in this book.

It was the Koffee 'N Toastmasters Club in Redlands, California, where I overcame my fear of public speaking. And it was Terry

McCann, former executive director of Toastmasters International, who helped launch my career in training and development.

A few of my stories involved intensive indoor workshops that I attended. Those were provided by the Lifespring organization. Although controversial and now defunct, I personally got a lot out of their programs.

Coy Theobolt was involved in three of my stories, including *The Sailing Trip from Hell* and *What's a Man Walk*. He will always be an inspiration to me. Dave Zarou started the Man Walk and continues to make a difference in the lives of men.

My mastermind group featured in *The Greater Yes* story will always hold a special place in my heart. Thank you, Mark Lipsitt, Lisa Carroll, and Crystal Thomas.

When my dog Bailey was attacked, people stepped up to support me. I want to thank my HR colleagues at DU for being there for me and embracing Bailey as a member of our team. And if it wasn't for the help of Wanda McKnight and Roger Jensen on Coyote Street, I don't know if Bailey would have survived. They were lifesavers. Taylor and Akeem Makeen became Bailey's second family (and mine) after I moved to Wash Park, making Bailey the most spoiled and happiest dog ever!

One of my fondest memories will always be the six years I was on talk radio. It was the radio show that inspired me to first blog and begin telling my stories. I especially want to thank cohosts Steve Sorensen and Lisa Samuels Dunning. It was such a high to be a part of that show. And thank you Larry "Hoss" Andrews and mileHIradio.com for making it happen.

Ken Pinnock has been a colleague and friend for years. He was instrumental in cocreating the Eight Simple Rules to Managing Conflict video series and a big supporter of this book project.

Char Burgess and Susan Hunter Hancock were the two deans who believed in me and gave me a second chance early in my career. I'll always be grateful to both of them.

Probably the best boss I ever had was Justin Carroll. He was like an older brother to me.

John Heider may have been the star of the *Let Go of My Ego* story, but it was the program facilitators—Pat Pendleton, Ted Lothamer, and Wayne Tittes Sr.—who demonstrated master facilitation every time we met during our nine months together at People House.

Special thanks to Carol Duggan, my former running buddy, who was instrumental in helping me complete my marathon. I'd also like to thank Shannon Scott for turning me on to the park benches at Wash Park. And speaking of park benches, a shout out to Berith Jacobsen for telling me her story about how my park bench impacted her life.

Writing a book is the easy part; the hard part is everything else. I want to thank Barbara Brooks of Flamingo Strategies LLC for her editing, Eric Weber for the cover portrait, taken at my park bench in Wash Park, Shelly Spaulding for the back cover photo taken during one of the Leading From Within programs, Erik Hofstetter of Creative Visions for designing the book cover, and Michele DeFilippo of 1106 Design for designing the book's interior.

Lastly, thank you, Terry & Margie Lewis, for your ongoing friendship and support over the years. I look forward to much more golf and Mexican restaurants.

CPSIA information can be obtained
at www.ICGtesting.com
Printed in the USA
LVHW101001061019
633315LV00009B/204/P